It's another Quality Book from CGP

This book is for anyone doing AQA Modular GCSE Maths at Higher Level.

It contains lots of tricky questions designed to make you sweat — because that's the only way you'll get any better.

It's also got some daft bits in to try and make the whole experience at least vaguely entertaining for you.

What CGP is all about

Our sole aim here at CGP is to produce the highest quality books — carefully written, immaculately presented and dangerously close to being funny.

Then we work our socks off to get them out to you — at the cheapest possible prices.

d1

Contents

Don't panic! We haven't forgotten about Modules Two and Four — they're coursework modules, so you don't need to revise them for the exams.

Module One

Probability 1
Frequency Tables 4
Grouped Frequency 6
Cumulative Frequency 7
Histograms 8
Scatter Graphs 9
Sampling 10
Time Series 11

Module Three

Numbers 12
Factors and Primes 13
Powers (Indices) 14
Rational and Irrational Numbers and Surds 15
Decimals 16
Standard Index Form 17
Algebra — The Basics 19
Fractions 20
Percentages 22
Growth and Decay 24
Ratios 25
Calculator Buttons 26
Conversion Factors 28
Metric and Imperial Units 29
Estimating 30
Rounding Off 31
Direct and Inverse Proportion 32
Plotting Curves 34
Plotting Straight-Line Graphs 35
Solving Equations Using Graphs 37

Module Five

Sequences 40
Algebra 42
Algebraic Fractions 43
Speed, Distance and Time 45
Solving Equations 47
Rearranging Formulas 48
Inequalities 49
Factorising Quadratics 51
The Quadratic Formula 52
Completing the Square 53
Simultaneous Equations 54
Trial and Improvement 56
Straight Lines 57
Straight-Line Graphs: $y = mx + c$ 58
Graphs to Recognise 60
Equations From Graphs 63
Transforming Graphs 64
D/T Graphs and V/T Graphs 65
Areas 68
Volumes 70
Length, Area and Volume 72
Circle Geometry 73
Loci and Constructions 75
The Four Transformations 77
Similarity and Enlargement 78
Vectors 80
Real-Life Vectors 81
Pythagoras' Theorem and Bearings 83
Trigonometry 86
The Sine and Cosine Rules 88
The Graphs of Sin, Cos and Tan 90
Angles of Any Size 92

Published by Coordination Group Publications Ltd.
Illustrated by Lex Ward and Ashley Tyson

Coordinated by June Hall and Mark Haslam

Contributors:
Gill Allen
JE Dodds
Mark Haslam
Claire Thompson
Dave Williams

Updated by:
Alison Chisholm
Ann Francis
Sharon Keeley
Tim Major
Mark Moody
Sam Norman
Alan Rix
Glenn Rogers
Bob Summers
Mark Turner

ISBN 1 84146 092 3

Groovy website: www.cgpbooks.co.uk

Printed by Elanders Hindson, Newcastle upon Tyne.
Clipart sources: CorelDRAW and VECTOR.

Probability

Q1 Charlton's cricket team had the results shown on the right over their last 20 matches.

W	W	L	D	D	W	W	L	W	L
D	L	L	D	W	D	W	W	L	L

a) Complete the frequency table.

Outcome	Frequency
W	
D	
L	

b) Charlton reasons that since there are 3 possible results for any match, the probability that the next match will be drawn (D) is $\frac{1}{3}$.
Explain why Charlton is wrong.

c) Suggest a value for the probability of a draw based on the past performance of Charlton's team.

Q2 **a)** What is the probability of randomly selecting either a black ace or black king from an ordinary pack of playing cards?

b) If the entire suit of clubs is removed from a pack of cards, what is the probability of randomly selecting a red 7?

c) If all the 7's are also removed from the pack of cards, what is the probability of randomly selecting the 4 of diamonds?

Q3 For the roulette wheel shown, the probability of the ball landing on each of the numbers is given in the table below.

Number	1	2	3	4	5	6
Probability	$\frac{1}{6}$	$\frac{1}{3}$	$\frac{1}{6}$	$\frac{1}{12}$	$\frac{1}{12}$	$\frac{1}{6}$

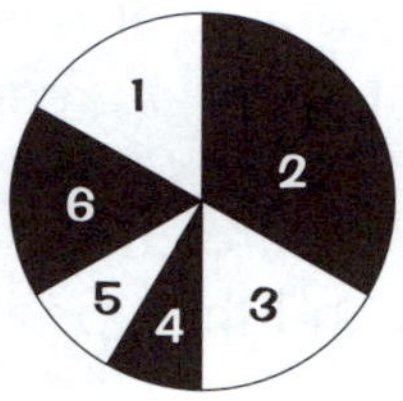

a) Find the probability of landing on an even number.

b) What is the probability of landing on black?

c) Why is the probability of landing on a white or a 3 not $\frac{5}{12} + \frac{1}{6}$?

Q4 The notepad below shows orders for 4 different sorts of rice at a certain Indian restaurant. Based on this data, what is the probability that the next order of rice is:

a) for pilau rice?

b) for spicy mushroom or special fried rice?

c) not for boiled rice?

boiled	20
pilau	24
spicy mushroom	10
special fried	6

Probability

The AND / OR Rules can get quite confusing, so get them drummed into your head before the Exam...

For AND, you MULTIPLY (along the branches)
For OR, you ADD (the end results)

See — told you it was confusing.

Q5 There are 2 fair spinners: one with 3 sides numbered 1, 2, 3, and the other with 7 sides numbered 1, 2, 3, 4, 5, 6, 7.

a) If both are spun together, list all the possible outcomes.

b) Complete the following table showing the sum of the 2 numbers for each outcome.

	1	2	3	4	5	6	7
1							
2							
3							

c) What is the probability that the sum is 6?
d) What is the probability that the sum is even?
e) What is the probability that the sum is greater than or equal to 8?
f) What is the probability that the sum is less than 8?
g) Explain how you can work out the probability in part **f)** without using the table.

Q6 3 balls are drawn at random, without replacement, from a bag containing 4 green balls and 3 red balls.

a) Complete the tree diagram below showing all the possible outcomes and their probabilities.

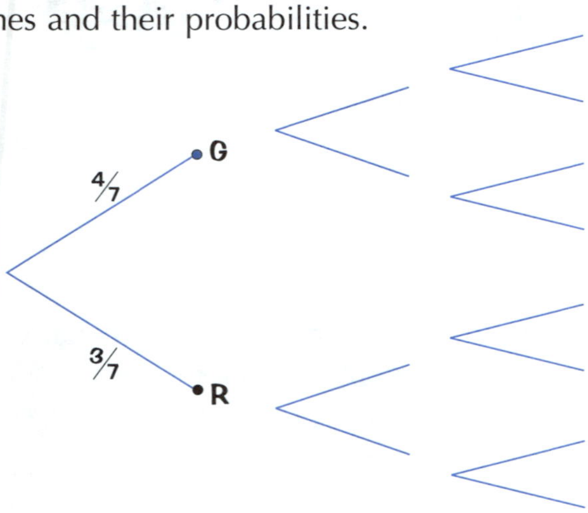

b) What is the probability that exactly 2 green balls are drawn?
c) What is the probability that the last ball drawn is the same colour as the first?

They're getting easier already, aren't they...

Probability

Don't forget the "at least" trick — if you're looking for P(at least ...) happening, all you need to do is find 1 – P(not ...). If you do it the other way round it'll take ages, believe me.

Q7 An unbiased dice in the shape of a tetrahedron has corners numbered 1, 2, 3, 4. To win a game with this dice, you must throw a 4. At each go you have a maximum of 3 attempts.

a) Using a tree diagram, calculate the probability of winning with the second throw of the first go.

b) What is the probability of winning on the first go?

Q8 How many times must you roll an ordinary 6-sided dice for the probability of getting at least one 6 to be more than 0.5?

Q9 3 coins are drawn at random, without replacement, from a piggy bank containing 7 pound coins and 4 twenty-pence pieces.

a) Draw a tree diagram showing all possible outcomes and their probabilities.

b) Find the probability that the first coin selected is different in value from the third.

c) Find the probability that less than £1.50 is drawn altogether.

Q10 Trevor and his 2 brothers and 5 friends are seated at random in a row of 8 seats at the cinema. What is the probability that Trevor has one brother on his immediate left and one on his immediate right?

Q11 Fabrizio is playing roulette. There are five sectors to the wheel, labelled 1 to 5. He wants to know if the wheel is biased before he bets any money. He records how many times he spins a 3.

Number of Spins	10	20	30	50	100
Number of 3's Spun	2	5	8	14	27

a) Calculate the relative frequency after 10, 20, 30, 50 and 100 spins.

b) Which probability estimate is likely to be most accurate?

c) Is the roulette wheel biased?

Frequency Tables

Q1 130 female bus drivers were weighed to the nearest kg.
Calculate:

a) the median weight
b) the modal weight
c) the mean weight, by first completing the table.

Weight (kg)	Frequency	Weight × Frequency
51	40	
52	30	
53	45	
54	10	
55	5	

You've got to be able to do these in both row and column form, because they could give you either one. There's no real difference, and the rules are still the same.

Q2 A travel company logs all calls to their sales desk. The number of calls per day received by the sales desk over a given year are shown below.

No. of Calls	10 and under	11	12	13	14	15	16 and over
No. of Days	110	70	120	27	18	12	8

a) Find the median number of calls.
b) Find the modal number of calls.

Q3 A student has classes in Mathematics (M), English (E), French (F), Art (A) and Science (S).
Her timetable is:

Monday	S S E E A
Tuesday	E M M A A
Wednesday	S M E F F
Thursday	F E E A S
Friday	M M E S S

a) Complete the following frequency table for a week's lessons:

Subject	M	E	F	A	S
Frequency					

b) Calculate the number of French lessons that the student will attend during a 12-week term.
c) What is the modal lesson?

Frequency Tables

Q4 20 pupils were asked to estimate the length (to the nearest m) of their gardens. Put the estimates in the frequency table below.

10, 8, 6, 4, 10, 8, 0, 14, 12, 8, 10, 6, 1, 6, 10, 8, 6, 6, 8, 8

a) Find the mode of the data.
b) Find the median of the data.
c) State the range of the data.

Length (m)	4 and under	6	8	10	12	14 and over
Frequency						

Q5 Using the computerised till in a shoe shop, the manager can work out what stock to order from the previous week's sales. Opposite is the tabularised printout for last week for men's shoes.

Shoe size	5	6	7	8	9	10	11
frequency	9	28	56	70	56	28	9

a) The mean, mode and median for this data can be compared. For each of the following statements decide whether it is true or false.
i) The mode for this data is 70.
ii) The mean is greater than the median for this distribution.
iii) The mean, median and mode are all equal in this distribution.

b) What percentage of customers bought shoes of the mean size from last week's sales data:
i) 30% **ii)** 70% **iii)** 0.273% or **iv)** 27.3%?

Q6 A survey is carried out in a small village to find out how many bedrooms the houses have. The frequency table displays the results.

No. of bedrooms	1	2	3	4	5
Frequency	3	5	6	2	4

Find the mean, mode and median of the data.

Q7 A tornado has struck the hamlet of Moose-on-the-Wold. Many houses have had windows broken. The frequency table shows the devastating effects.

No. of windows broken per house	0	1	2	3	4	5	6
Frequency	5	3	4	11	13	7	2

a) Calculate the modal number of broken windows.
b) Calculate the median number of broken windows.
c) Calculate the mean number of broken windows.

Grouped Frequency

Q1 The weights of 18 newly felled trees are noted below in kg:

272.7	333.2	251.0	246.5	328.0	259.6	200.2	312.8
344.3	226.8	362.0	348.3	256.1	232.9	309.7	398.0
284.5	327.4						

a) Complete the frequency table.

Weight (kg)	Tally	Frequency	Mid-Interval	Frequency × Mid-Interval
200 – 249				
250 – 299				
300 – 349				
350 – 399				

b) Estimate the mean weight using the frequency table.
c) What is the modal group?

Q2 The speeds of 32 skiers at a certain corner of a downhill course are tabulated below.

Speed (km/h)	40 – 44	45 – 49	50 – 54	55 – 59	60 – 64
Frequency	4	8	10	7	3
Mid-Interval					
Frequency × Mid-Interval					

a) By completing the frequency table, estimate the mean speed.
b) How many skiers were travelling at less than 54.5 km/h?
c) How many skiers were travelling more than 49.5 km/h?

Q3 48 numbers are recorded below:

0.057	0.805	0.056	0.979	0.419	0.160	0.534	0.763
0.642	0.569	0.773	0.055	0.349	0.892	0.664	0.136
0.528	0.792	0.085	0.546	0.549	0.908	0.639	0.000
0.614	0.478	0.421	0.472	0.292	0.579	0.542	0.356
0.070	0.890	0.883	0.333	0.033	0.323	0.544	0.668
0.094	0.049	0.049	0.999	0.632	0.700	0.983	0.356

a) Transfer the data into the frequency table.

Number	$0 \leqslant n < 0.2$	$0.2 \leqslant n < 0.4$	$0.4 \leqslant n < 0.6$	$0.6 \leqslant n < 0.8$	$0.8 \leqslant n < 1$
Tally					
Frequency					
Mid-Interval					
Frequency × Mid-Interval					

b) Which is the modal class?
c) Which group contains the median?
d) Estimate the mean value.

Cumulative Frequency

Some of these questions ask you to draw a box plot as well. Remember, it's much easier to put it <u>directly under the cumulative frequency curve</u> you've just drawn. Then you can extend the lines for the median and quartiles, rather than having to remeasure them.

Q1 Using the cumulative frequency curve, read off the:

a) median
b) lower quartile
c) upper quartile
d) interquartile range.

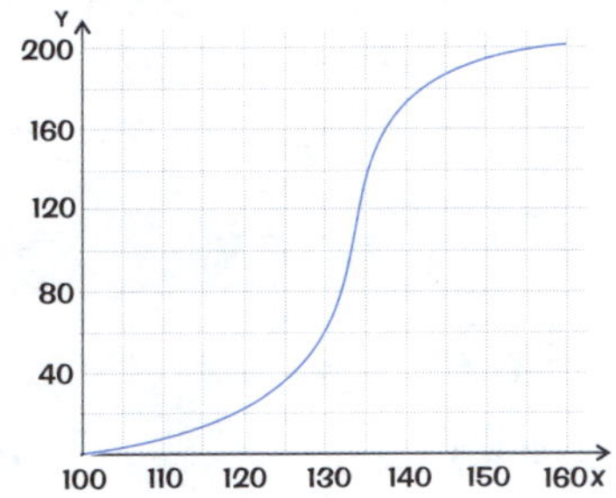

Q2 40 pupils have taken an exam and their marks are recorded in the frequency table below.

Mark (%)	$0 \leqslant m < 20$	$20 \leqslant m < 40$	$40 \leqslant m < 60$	$60 \leqslant m < 80$	$80 \leqslant m < 100$
Frequency	2	12	18	5	3
Cumulative Frequency					

a) Complete the table and plot the cumulative frequency curve.
b) What is the value of the lower quartile?
c) What is the interquartile range?
d) What is the median mark?

Q3 A group of parents carried out a survey on the price of trainers, then tabulated the results.

Prices of Trainers (£)	0 – 29	30 – 59	60 – 89	90 – 119	120 – 149	150 – 179
Frequency	4	18	24	20	11	3
Cumulative Frequency						
Mid-Interval						
Frequency × Mid-Interval						

a) Fill in the rest of the table.
b) How many pairs of trainers did the parents investigate?
c) Plot the cumulative frequency curve.
d) Which is higher, the mean or the median price?

Q4 The top 100 scores for a board game are presented in the table below.

Score	31 – 40	41 – 50	51 – 60	61 – 70	71 – 80	81 – 90	91 – 100
Frequency	4	12	21	32	19	8	4
Cumulative Frequency							

a) What is the modal group?
b) Which group contains the median score?
c) By plotting the cumulative frequency curve, estimate the actual value of the median score.
d) Find the interquartile range.
e) Draw the box plot.

Histograms

It's the <u>size that counts</u>... You've got to look at the <u>area</u> of the bars, which means looking at the <u>width</u> as well as the height.

Q1 The histogram below represents the age distribution of people that watch outdoor bog snorkelling. Given that there are 24 people in the 40-55 age range, find the number of people in all the other age ranges.

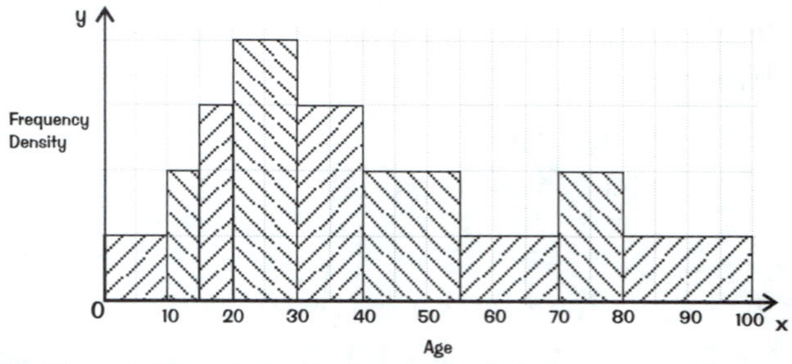

Q2 The weight of honey collected from several beehives is tabulated below:

a) Complete the frequency table by calculating the frequency densities.
b) Draw a histogram to represent this data.
c) Use your histogram to estimate the number of beehives producing more than 6 kg of honey.

Weight (kg)	0 – 2	3 – 4	5 – 7	8 – 9	10 – 15
Frequency	3	2	6	9	12
Frequency density					

Q3 The lifetimes of 96 microwaves are tabulated below:

Lifetime (years)	$0 \leqslant L < 2$	$2 \leqslant L < 4$	$4 \leqslant L < 6$	$6 \leqslant L < 8$	$8 \leqslant L < 10$	$10 \leqslant L < 12$
Frequency	15	22	36	9	10	4
Frequency density						
Mid-Interval						
Frequency × Mid-Interval						

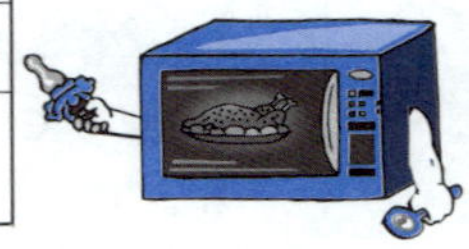

a) Complete the frequency table.
b) Estimate the mean lifetime.
c) Which group contains the median value?
d) How many lifetimes are outside the modal group?
e) Draw a histogram and use it to determine the number of microwaves with lifetimes shorter than 5 years.

Q4 A group of sixth formers took part in a survey to see how much time they spent watching TV each week.

a) Complete the table by filling in the frequency density column.
b) How many students took part in the survey?
c) Represent the data as a histogram.
d) Estimate the number of students that watch more than 7, but less than 13 hours each week.

No. of hours	Frequency	Frequency density
0 – 1	6	
2 – 3	13	
4 – 5	15	
6 – 8	9	
9 – 10	23	
11 – 15	25	
16 – 20	12	

Scatter Graphs

A SCATTER GRAPH is just a load of points on a graph that end up in a bit of a mess, rather than in a nice line or curve. There's a fancy word to say how much of a mess they're in — it's CORRELATION.

Q1 Match the following diagrams with the most appropriate descriptive label.

Labels: (P) Strong positive correlation (S) Moderate negative correlation
(Q) Exact negative correlation (T) Medium correlation
(R) Little or no correlation (U) Exact positive correlation.

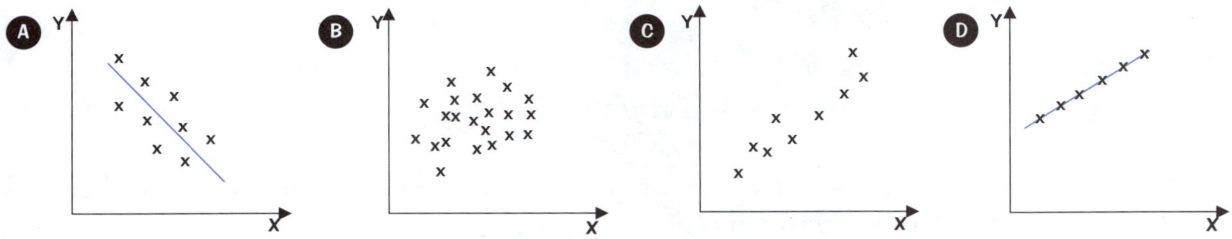

Q2 8 friends are comparing heights and shoe sizes to see if they are correlated.
The data is tabulated below:

Height	4'6"	4'8"	5'2"	5'5"	5'8"	5'10"	6'	6'6"
Shoe size	4	5	4.5	5	6	8	9	12

a) Plot the points on a scatter graph.
b) Are the points positively or negatively correlated?
c) By fitting an appropriate line, estimate the shoe size of another friend who is 6'2".

Q3 Janine is convinced that more expensive cookery books contain more pages.
To test out her theory, she has compiled the following table:

Price	£4.25	£5.00	£4.75	£6.25	£7.50	£8.25	£4.75	£5.00	£6.75	£3.25	£3.75
No. of pages	172	202	118	184	278	328	158	138	268	84	98

a) Draw a scatter graph to represent this information.
b) Draw in a line of best fit.
c) Use your line to estimate the price of a book containing 250 pages.

Q4 A local electrical store has kept a log of the number of CD players sold at each price:

Price (£)	£80	£150	£230	£310	£380	£460
No. Sold	27	24	22	19	17	15

a) Draw this information as a scatter graph, using suitable axes.
b) Draw a line of best fit and use it to estimate the number of CD players the shopkeeper could expect to sell for £280.
c) Is the data positively or negatively correlated?

Sampling

Q1 Give a definition of:

a) random sampling

b) systematic sampling

c) stratified sampling

You've got to know the main types of sampling — have a go at Q1, and if you can't get it right, keep trying till you can.

You've also got to be able to spot problems and criticise sampling techniques — basically, if you think it's a load of rubbish, you get the chance to say why.

Q2 Give a reason why the following methods of sampling are poor:

a) a survey carried out inside a newsagents concluded that 80% of the population buy a daily newspaper

b) a phone poll conducted at 11 am on a Sunday morning revealed that less than 2% of the population regularly go to church

c) 60% of the population were estimated to watch the 9 o'clock news each evening after a survey was carried out at a bridge club.

Q3 Decide which of the following questions (if any) are suitable for a survey to find which of five desserts (cheesecake, fruit salad, sherry trifle, knickerbocker glory and chocolate cake) people like the most. Give a reason for each of your answers.

a) Do you like cheesecake, fruit salad, sherry trifle, knickerbocker glory or chocolate cake?

b) How often do you eat dessert?

c) Which is your favourite out of: cheesecake; fruit salad; sherry trifle; knickerbocker glory; chocolate cake?

d) What is your favourite dessert?

e) Is your favourite dessert: cheesecake; fruit salad; sherry trifle; knickerbocker glory; chocolate cake; none of these?

Q4 A newspaper contained the following article regarding the amount of exercise teenagers take outside school.

a) Suggest 3 questions that you could use in a survey to find out whether this is true at your school.

b) At a particular school there are 300 pupils in each of years 7 to 11. There are approximately equal numbers of girls and boys. Describe how you would select 10% of the pupils for a stratified sample which is representative of all the pupils at the school.

Time Series

Time Series — don't you just love 'em. These little horrors are pretty important, and could easily raise their ugly head in the Exam. Do yourself a favour and practise them.

Q1 Which of the following sets of measurements form time series?

a) The average rainfall in Cumbria, measured each day for a year.

b) The daily rainfall in European capital cities on Christmas Day, 2000.

c) The shoe size of everybody in Class 6C on September 1st, 2001.

d) My shoe size (measured every month) from when I was twelve months old to when I was fourteen years old.

Q2 **a)** Which two of the following time series are seasonal, and which two are not seasonal?

A

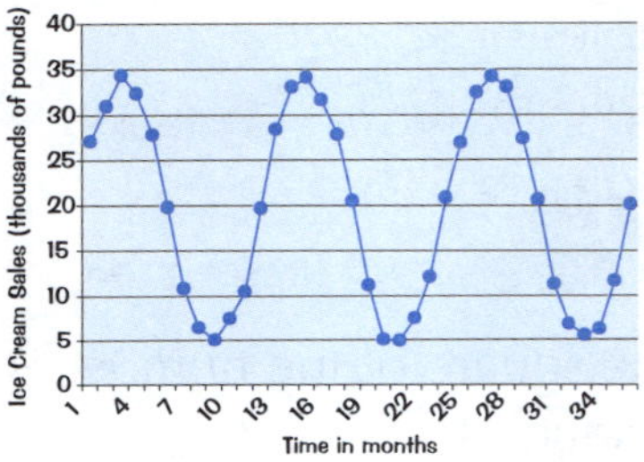

B

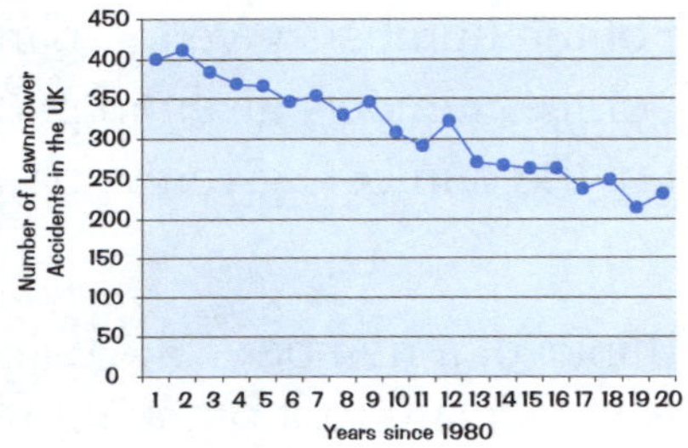

C

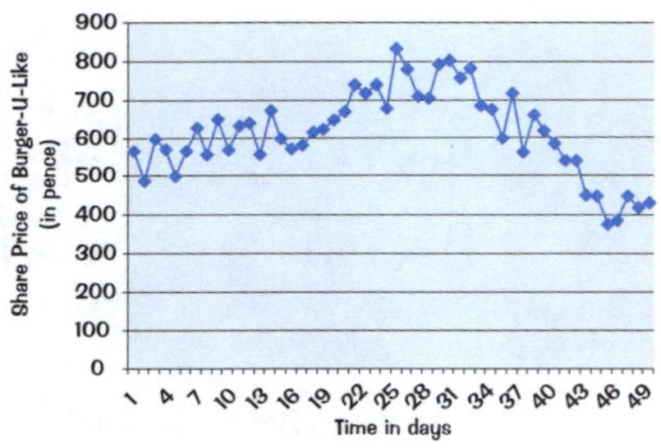

D

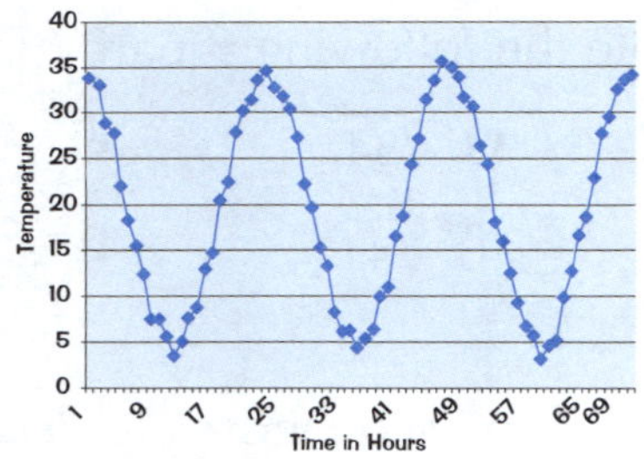

b) What are the periods of the time series which are seasonal?

c) Describe the trends in the time series which are **not** seasonal.

Q3 The following table shows the value of a knitwear company's sock sales in the years 1998-2000. The sales figures are given in thousands of pounds.

Time	Sales
Spring 1998	404
Summer 1998	401
Autumn 1998	411
Winter 1998	420
Spring 1999	416
Summer 1999	409
Autumn 1999	419
Winter 1999	424
Spring 2000	416
Summer 2000	413
Autumn 2000	427
Winter 2000	440

a) Plot the figures on a graph with time on the horizontal axis and sales on the vertical axis.

b) Calculate a 4-point moving average to smooth the series. Write the averages in the boxes provided.

c) Plot the moving average on the same axes as your original graph.

d) Describe the trend of the sales figures.

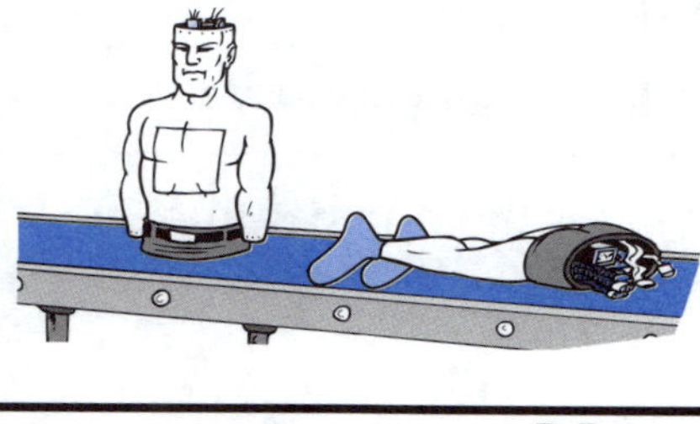

Numbers

There are four special number sequences that you really need to know: EVEN, ODD, SQUARE and CUBE NUMBERS.

Q1 The number one is the first odd number. It is also the first square number and the first cube number. Which is greatest, the third odd number, the third square number, or the third cube number?

Q2 **a)** Write down the first five cube numbers.
b) Which of the numbers given in part **a)** are multiples of 2?
c) Which of the numbers given in part **a)** are multiples of 3?
d) Which of the numbers given in part **a)** are multiples of 4?
e) Which of the numbers given in part **a)** are multiples of 5?

Q3 Sarah thinks of a number. She calculates that the square of the number is 256. What is the square root of the number she's thinking of?

Q4 Estimate the following square roots, to 1 d.p.:

a) $\sqrt{48}$ **c)** $\sqrt{84}$ **e)** $\sqrt{200}$ **g)** $\sqrt{17}$ **i)** $\sqrt{34}$ **k)** $\sqrt{180}$

b) $\sqrt{118}$ **d)** $\sqrt{41}$ **f)** $\sqrt{30}$ **h)** $\sqrt{98}$ **j)** $\sqrt{150}$ **l)** $\sqrt{140}$

Q5 The following sequences are described in words. Write down their first four terms.
a) The prime numbers starting from 17.
b) The squares of odd numbers starting from $9^2 = 81$.

Q6 Bryan and Sue were playing a guessing game. Sue thought of a number between 1 and 100 which Bryan had to guess. Bryan was allowed to ask five questions, which are listed with Sue's responses in the table below.

Bryan's Questions	Sue's Responses
Is it prime?	No
Is it odd?	No
Is it less than 50?	Yes
Is it a multiple of 3?	Yes
Is it a multiple of 7?	Yes

What is the number that Sue thought of?

Factors and Primes

This is real basic stuff — you just have to know your times tables. And your primes, of course...

Q1 1 3 6 9 12

From the numbers above, write down:

a) a multiple of 4
b) the prime number
c) two square numbers
d) three factors of 27
e) two numbers P and Q that satisfy both P = 2Q and P = $\sqrt{144}$

Q2 Find the least common multiple of: **a)** 5 and 9 **b)** 4 and 6 **c)** 4, 6 and 8
Find the highest common factor of: **d)** 26 and 52 **e)** 26, 39 and 52

Q3 **a)** List the first five odd numbers.
b) If added together, what is their total?
c) Express your answer to **b)** as a product of prime factors.

Q4 **a)** List the first five prime numbers.
b) If added together, what is their total?
c) Express your answer to **b)** as a product of prime factors.

Q5 Using any or all of the figures **1, 2, 5, 9** write down:

a) the smallest prime number
b) a prime number greater than 20
c) a prime number between 10 and 20
d) two prime numbers whose sum is 21
e) a number that is not prime.

Remember — 1 is not a prime. Look, it just isn't, OK.

Q6 **a)** In the ten by ten square opposite, ring all the prime numbers. (The first three have been done for you.)
b) Among the prime numbers between 10 and 100, find three which are still prime when their digits are reversed.
c) Give a reason for 27 not being a prime number.

1	(2)	(3)	4	(5)	6	7	8	9	10
11	12	13	14	15	16	17	18	19	20
21	22	23	24	25	26	27	28	29	30
31	32	33	34	35	36	37	38	39	40
41	42	43	44	45	46	47	48	49	50
51	52	53	54	55	56	57	58	59	60
61	62	63	64	65	66	67	68	69	70
71	72	73	74	75	76	77	78	79	80
81	82	83	84	85	86	87	88	89	90
91	92	93	94	95	96	97	98	99	100

Q7 What is the largest prime less than 300?

Q8 How many prime numbers are even?

This stuff keeps coming up in the Exam — so make sure you can check if a number's prime or not. It's actually dead easy — check out the method in the Revision Guide.

Powers (Indices)

Hang on there. Before you try this page, make sure you know the seven rules for powers — you'll find them on P.19 of the Revision Guide, or you could just ask Teach.

The small number is called the power or index number. Remember the plural of index is indices.

$5^4 = 5 \times 5 \times 5 \times 5 =$ ______
we say "five to the power four"

$8^3 = 8 \times 8 \times 8 =$ ______
we say "eight to the power three" or "eight cubed"

To save time try using the power button on your calculator x^y y^x

eg. 5 x^y 4 =
8 x^y 3 =

Q1 Complete the following:

a) $2^4 = 2 \times 2 \times 2 \times 2 =$
b) $10^3 = 10 \times 10 \times 10 =$
c) $3^5 = 3 \times \ldots \quad =$
d) $4^6 = 4 \times \quad =$
e) $1^9 = 1 \times \quad =$
f) $5^6 = 5 \times \quad =$

Q2 Simplify the following:

a) $2 \times 2 \times 2 \times 2 \times 2 \times 2 \times 2 \times 2$
b) $12 \times 12 \times 12 \times 12 \times 12$
c) $x \times x \times x \times x \times x$
d) $m \times m \times m$
e) $y \times y \times y \times y$
f) $z \times z \times z \times z \times z \times z$

Q3 Complete the following (the first one has been done for you):

a) $10^2 \times 10^3 = (10 \times 10) \times (10 \times 10 \times 10) = 10^5$
b) $10^3 \times 10^4 = \quad =$
c) $10^4 \times 10^2 = \quad =$
d) $10^5 \times 10^3 = \quad =$
e) What is the <u>quick method</u> for writing down the final result in **b)**, **c)** and **d)**?

Easy — you'll have learnt this from your seven rules of powers.

Q4 Complete (the first one has been done for you):

a) $2^4 \div 2^2 = \frac{(2\times2\times2\times2)}{(2\times2)} = 2^2$
b) $2^5 \div 2^2 = \frac{(2\times2\times2\times2\times2)}{(2\times2)} =$
c) $4^5 \div 4^3 = \frac{(4\times4\times4\times4\times4)}{\quad} =$
d) $8^5 \div 8^2 = \quad =$
e) What is the quick method for writing down the final result in **b)**, **c)** and **d)**?

Q5 Which of the following are <u>true</u>?

a) $2^4 \times 2^6 = 2^{10}$
b) $2^2 \times 2^3 \times 2^4 = 2^9$
c) $2^3 \times 2^2 = 2^6$
d) $4^{10} \times 4^4 \times 4^2 = 4^{18}$
e) $2^1 \times 2^3 \times 2^4 = 2^8$
f) $10^4 \times 10^2 = 10^8$
g) $2^{20} \div 2^5 = 2^4$
h) $3^{12} \div 3^4 = 3^8$
i) $4^6 \div 4^4 = 4^2$
j) $10^{20} \div 10^3 = 10^{17}$
k) $4^6 \div (4^2 \times 4^3) = 4^1$
l) $9^2 \times (9^{30} \div 9^{25}) = 9^{10}$

Q6 Remove the brackets from the following and express each as a single power:

a) $(3^4 \times 3^2) \div (3^6 \times 3^3)$
b) $(4^{10} \times 4^{12}) \times 4^3$
c) $10^2 \div (10^3 \times 10^{12})$
d) $(3^6)^{-2}$
e) $4^2 \times 4^{-1} \times 4^6 \times (4^2 \div 4^3)$
f) $(5^2 \times 5^3) \div (5^6 \div 5^4)$

Rational and Irrational Numbers and Surds

Well, to be honest, I think the idea of rational and irrational numbers is a bit odd. Basically, a rational number is either a whole number or one you can write as a fraction. An irrational number... you guessed it... is not whole and can't be written as a fraction.

Q1 Write down a rational number and an irrational number both greater than $\sqrt{5}$ and less than 5.

Q2 Give an example of two different irrational numbers, x and y, where $\frac{x}{y}$ is a rational number.

Q3 Give an example of two different irrational numbers, x and y, where xy is a rational number.

Q4 Write down a value of x for which $x^{\frac{1}{2}}$ is:

a) irrational
b) rational.

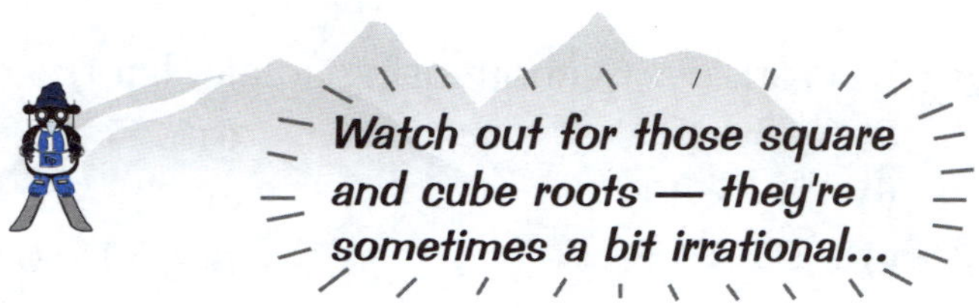

Q5 Which of the following powers of $\sqrt{3}$ are rational and which are irrational?

a) $(\quad)^1$
b) $(\quad)^2$
c) $(\quad)^3$
d) $(\quad)^4$

Q6 If $x = 2\sqrt{5}$, $y = 5$ and $z = 5\sqrt{2}$, which of the following expressions are rational and which are irrational? (show working)

a) x^5 **b)** x^2yz^2 **c)** $x\sqrt{5}$ **d)** $xy + z^2$

Q7 Simplify:

a) $\sqrt{5}\times\sqrt{3}$ **b)** $\frac{\sqrt{20}}{\sqrt{5}}$ **c)** $\sqrt{4}-\sqrt{1}$ **d)** $\left(\frac{\sqrt{5}}{\sqrt{2}}\right)^2$

e) $(\sqrt{x})^2$ **f)** $\sqrt{x^2}$ **g)** $\sqrt{8}\times\sqrt{8}$ **h)** $\sqrt{18}-\sqrt{9}$

Q8 Rationalise the denominators of the following expressions, and then simplify if necessary.

a) $\frac{1}{\sqrt{2}}$ **b)** $\frac{2}{\sqrt{8}}$ **c)** $\frac{a}{\frac{\sqrt{40}}{2}}$ **d)** $\frac{x}{\sqrt{xy}}$

e) $\frac{1}{1+\sqrt{2}}$ **f)** $\frac{6}{3+\sqrt{3}}$ **g)** $\frac{2}{1+\sqrt{6}}$ **h)** $\frac{5+\sqrt{5}}{5-\sqrt{5}}$

Remember: rationalising the denominator means getting rid of the square root sign on the bottom of a fraction.

Decimals

Q1 Write the following fractions as decimals:

a) $\frac{3}{10}$ **b)** $\frac{37}{100}$ **c)** $\frac{2}{5}$ **d)** $\frac{3}{8}$ **e)** $\frac{14}{8}$

Q2 Work out:

a) 33.9 × 10
b) 0.32 × 100
c) 2.3902 × 1000
d) 64.9 × 10
e) 122.6 × 100
f) 5.29 × 1000

You just shift the decimal point along... this is too easy.

Q3 Calculate (without using a calculator):

a) 8.38 + 8.46
b) 14.77 + 0.13
c) 4.83 + 35.32
d) 5.79 – 0.98
e) 109.79 – 68.32
f) 1.22 – 3.40
g) 1.84 + 8.61 + 5.6
h) (1.40 – 0.29) – 7.33
i) 7.33 + 59.2 – 34.2

Q4 Work out (without using a calculator):

a) 6.75 × 5
b) 3.59 × 3.8
c) 8.05 × 111.11
d) 6.75 ÷ 5
e) 6.25 ÷ 2.5
f) 4.29 ÷ 0.066
g) 5 × 6.2 × 3.9
h) (2.5 ÷ 5) ÷ 0.1
i) 1.6 × 0.4 ÷ 0.2

Q5 Terri's motorbike travels 122.5 km on 3.5 litres of petrol.

a) How many kilometres per litre is this?
b) How far can Terri travel on 0.3 litres of petrol?
c) How much petrol does Terri need to travel 7 km?

Q6 Fill in the gaps in the following conversion table:

Fraction	Decimal
1/2	0.5
1/5	
	0.125
	1.6
4/16	
7/2	
	0.x
x/100	
3/20	
	0.45

***Decimals** are just another way of writing **fractions** — so it's easy to convert between the two...*

Q7 Write the following recurring decimals as fractions in their lowest form:

a) 0.666...
b) 0.444...
c) 0.888...
d) 0.808080...
e) 0.121212...
f) 0.545545545...
g) 0.753753753...
h) 0.156156156...

Q8 Write the following fractions as recurring decimals:

a) $\frac{5}{6}$
b) $\frac{7}{9}$
c) $\frac{7}{11}$
d) $\frac{47}{99}$
e) $\frac{10}{11}$
f) $\frac{29}{33}$
g) $\frac{478}{999}$
h) $\frac{5891}{9999}$

Standard Index Form

Write the numbers in Questions 1–4 in standard form.

Q1 The distance between Paris and Rome is 1476 km.

Q2 A billion = a thousand million   A trillion = a thousand billion or million million.

Q3 A light year is 9,460,000,000,000 km (approx).

Q4 Nautilus covered 69,138 miles before having to refuel.

Q5 A rectangular field is 24,700 cm by 15,000 cm. Write its perimeter in m in standard form.

Q6 The density of a liquid is 1.25×10^3 kg/m^3. What is the volume of 500 g of this liquid?

Q7 This table gives the diameter and distance from the Sun of some planets.

Planet	Distance from Sun (km)	Diameter (km)
Earth	1.5×10^8	1.3×10^4
Venus	1.085×10^8	1.2×10^4
Mars	2.28×10^8	6.8×10^3
Mercury	5.81×10^7	4.9×10^3
Jupiter	7.8×10^8	1.4×10^5
Neptune	4.52×10^9	4.9×10^4
Saturn	1.43×10^9	1.2×10^5

From the table write down which planet is:

a) smallest in diameter
b) largest in diameter
c) nearest to the Sun
d) furthest from the Sun.

Write down which planets are:

e) nearer to the Sun than the Earth
f) bigger in diameter than the Earth.

Q8 Quartz vibrates at about 2.5 million pulses each second.
Caesium vibrates at about 9,192,631,770 vibrations per second.

a) Write both these numbers in standard form.
b) Calculate the difference between the number of vibrations per second of caesium and quartz.

Q9 The distance of some cities from Calais is given in the table below.

City	distance in km from Calais
Amsterdam	360
Barcelona	1326
Hamburg	714
Helsinki	1867
Madrid	1558
Marseille	1011

a) Write all the distances in standard form.
Work out which city is:
b) closest to Calais
c) furthest from Calais
d) approximately twice as far from Calais as Hamburg.
e) What is the ratio of the distance between Calais and Barcelona to that between Calais and Madrid?

Q10 One hour = 60 minutes   One minute = 60 seconds
Write in standard form the number of seconds in an hour.

a) What is the speed in km/s of a plane flying at 8.7×10^2 km/h?
b) The speed of light is approximately 3.0×10^8 m/s. Write this in km/h.

Q11 The mass of the Moon is about 0.0123 times that of the Earth. If the mass of the Earth is 5.974×10^{21} tonnes, calculate the mass of the Moon to 3 s.f.

You may have noticed standard form is used a lot in science, so if you're a budding nuclear physicist, get learning. Oh, you're not. Well, you've still got to learn it. Sorry.

Standard Index Form

Writing very big (or very small) numbers gets a bit messy with all those zeros, if you don't use standard index form. But of course, the main reason for knowing about standard form is... you guessed it — it's in the Exam.

Q12 Write as ordinary numbers:

a) 3.56×10^1
b) 3.56×10^3
c) 3.56×10^{-1}
d) 3.56×10^4
e) 0.082×10^2
f) 0.082×10^{-2}
g) 0.082×10^1
h) 0.082×10^{-1}
i) 157×10^1
j) 157×10^{-3}
k) 157×10^3
l) 157×10^{-1}

Q13 Write in standard form:

a) 2.56
b) 25.6
c) 0.256
d) 25600
e) 95.2
f) 0.0952
g) 95 200
h) 0.000952
i) 4200
j) 0.0042
k) 42
l) 420

Q14 Write in standard form:

a) 34.7×10^1
b) 73.004
c) 0.005×10^3
d) 9183×10^2
e) 15 million
f) 937.1×10^4
g) 0.000075
h) 0.05×10^{-2}
i) 534×10^{-2}
j) 621.03
k) 149×10^2
l) 0.003×10^{-4}

Q15 Calculate and give your answers in standard form:

a) $(3.7 \times 10^2) \times (1.4 \times 10^4)$
b) $(0.5 \times 10^3) \times (8.1 \times 10^2)$
c) $(0.03 \times 10^{-1}) \times (5.6 \times 10^{-2})$
d) $(3.9 \times 10^2) \div (2.7 \times 10^1)$
e) $(0.7 \times 10^4) \div (1.5 \times 10^2)$
f) $(8.21 \times 10^5) \div (0.4 \times 10^3)$

Q16 Calculate and give your answers in standard form:

a) $(4.5 \times 10^2)^2$
b) $\sqrt{4.9 \times 10^3}$
c) $\dfrac{0.534 \times 10^{-1}}{2.3 \times 10^{-4}}$
d) $\dfrac{4 \times 10^{-2}}{8 \times 10^{-3}}$
e) $(2.86 \times 10^{-3})^2$
f) $\sqrt{0.36 \times 10^{-2}}$

Q17 Calculate the following, writing your answer as an ordinary decimal number:

a) $(2.4 \times 10^2) \div (1.5 \times 10^1)$
b) $(0.5 \times 10^{-1}) \times (3.2 \times 10^{-2})$
c) $(3.7 \times 10^4) \div (5.6 \times 10^3)$
d) $(0.03 \times 10^3) \times (0.71 \times 10^{-2})$
e) $256.3 \div (0.19 \times 10^2)$
f) $(2.76 \times 10^{-2}) \times 576$
g) $0.003 \times (2.4 \times 10^2)$
h) $(1.98 \times 10^{-4}) \div 0.0004$
i) $2{,}468 \times (0.9 \times 10^{-3})$
j) $(3.7 \times 10^{-5}) \div (1.5 \times 10^4)$

Don't forget that if it's a negative power, you move the decimal point the other way.

Algebra — The Basics

Q1 Work out the following temperature changes:

a) 20 °C to –7 °C
b) –10 °C to –32 °C
c) –17 °C to –5 °C
d) –3 °C to 15 °C
e) –31 °C to –16 °C
f) –5 °C to –17 °C

Q2 Which is larger and by how much?

a) –12 + 7 – 4 + 6 – 2 + 7 or **b)** –30 + 26 – 3 – 7 + 17

Q3 Simplify **a)** $4x - 5x + 3x - x + 2x - 7x$ **b)** $30y - 10y + 2y - 3y + 4y - 5y$

Q4 Find the value of xy and $\frac{x}{y}$ for each of the following:

a) $x = -100$ $y = 10$
b) $x = 24$ $y = -4$
c) $x = -48$ $y = -3$
d) $x = 0$ $y = -4$

Q5 Find the value of $(a - b) \div (c + d)$ when $a = 10$, $b = -26$, $c = -5$ and $d = -4$.

Q6 Simplify the following:

a) $2x \times -3y$
b) $-8a \times 2b$
c) $-4x \times -2x$
d) $4p \times -4p$
e) $-30x \div -3y$
f) $50x \div -5y$
g) $10x \div -2y$
h) $-30x \div -10x$
i) $40ab \div -10ab$
j) $70x^2 \div -7x^2$
k) $-36x^2 \div -9x$
l) $40y^2 \div -5y$

Q7 Simplify the following by collecting like terms together:

a) $3x^2 + 4x + 12x^2 - 5x$
b) $14x^2 - 10x - x^2 + 5x$
c) $12 - 4x^2 + 10x - 3x^2 + 2x$
d) $20abc + 12ab + 10bac + 4bc$
e) $8pq + 7p + q + 10qp - q + p$
f) $15ab - 10a + b - 7a + 2ba$
g) $4pq - 14p - 8q + p - q + 8p$
h) $13x^2 + 4x^2 - 5y^2 + y^2 - x^2$
i) $11ab + 2cd - ba - 13dc + abc$
j) $3x^2 + 4xy + 2y^2 - z^2 + 2xy - y^2 - 5x^2$

Q8 The rectangular bar of chocolate shown consists of 20 small rectangular pieces. The size of a small rectangular piece of chocolate is 2 cm by x cm.

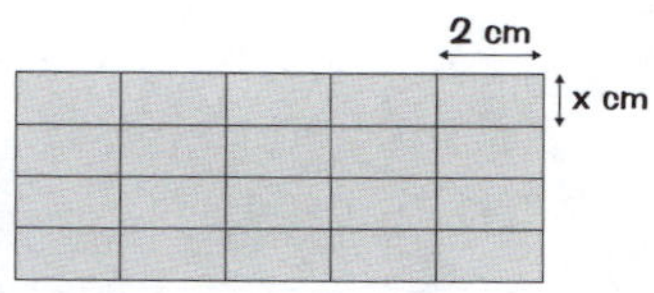

a) Write down an expression for the perimeter of the whole bar.
b) Write down an expression for the area of the whole bar.
c) If I ate 6 small rectangular pieces of chocolate, what is the area of the remaining piece?

Q9 For each of the large rectangles below, write down the area of each of the small rectangles and hence find an expression for the area of the large rectangle.

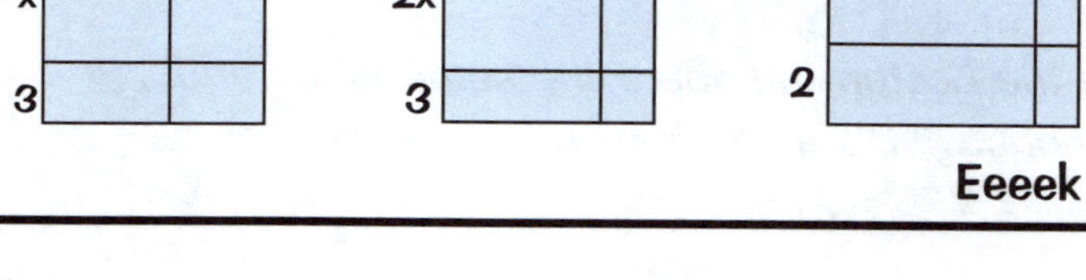

Eeeek — loads of questions...

Fractions

Q1 Evaluate the following, giving your answers as fractions in their lowest terms:

a) $\frac{1}{8}+\frac{1}{8}$ **c)** $\frac{3}{18}+\frac{1}{3}$ **e)** $1\frac{1}{4}+4\frac{1}{8}$

b) $\frac{1}{6}+\frac{2}{3}$ **d)** $1\frac{1}{4}+3\frac{1}{8}$ **f)** $\frac{9}{10}+\frac{9}{100}+\frac{1}{100}$

Q2 Evaluate the following, giving your answers as fractions in their lowest terms:

a) $\frac{1}{8}-\frac{1}{8}$ **c)** $\frac{3}{18}-\frac{1}{3}$ **e)** $1\frac{1}{8}-4\frac{1}{4}$

b) $\frac{2}{3}-\frac{1}{6}$ **d)** $3\frac{1}{8}-1\frac{1}{4}$ **f)** $\left(\frac{9}{10}-\frac{9}{100}\right)-\frac{1}{100}$

Q3 Carry out the following multiplications, giving your answers as fractions in their lowest terms:

a) $\frac{1}{8}\times\frac{1}{8}$ **c)** $\frac{3}{18}\times\frac{1}{3}$ **e)** $1\frac{1}{8}\times4\frac{1}{4}$

b) $\frac{1}{6}\times\frac{2}{3}$ **d)** $3\frac{1}{8}\times1\frac{1}{4}$ **f)** $\frac{9}{10}\times\frac{9}{100}\times\frac{1}{100}$

Q4 Carry out the following divisions, giving your answers as fractions in their lowest terms:

a) $\frac{1}{8}\div\frac{1}{8}$ **c)** $\frac{3}{18}\div\frac{1}{3}$ **e)** $1\frac{1}{8}\div4\frac{1}{4}$

b) $\frac{1}{6}\div\frac{2}{3}$ **d)** $3\frac{1}{8}\div1\frac{1}{4}$ **f)** $\left(\frac{9}{10}\div\frac{9}{100}\right)\div\frac{1}{100}$

Q5 Evaluate the following, giving your answers as fractions in their lowest terms:

a) $\frac{1}{2}+\frac{1}{4}$ **e)** $6\times\frac{2}{3}$ **i)** $3+\frac{8}{5}$

b) $\frac{2}{3}-\frac{1}{4}$ **f)** $\frac{4}{5}\div\frac{2}{3}$ **j)** $\frac{2}{3}\left(\frac{3}{4}+\frac{4}{5}\right)$

c) $\frac{1}{5}+\frac{2}{3}-\frac{2}{5}$ **g)** $\frac{5}{12}\times\frac{2}{3}$ **k)** $\left(\frac{1}{7}+\frac{3}{14}\right)\times\left(3-\frac{1}{5}\right)$

d) $5-\frac{1}{4}$ **h)** $\frac{5}{6}-\frac{7}{8}$ **l)** $\left(\frac{3}{4}-\frac{1}{5}\right)\div\left(\frac{7}{8}+\frac{1}{16}\right)$

Q6 Dwight scored 50 goals last season, 30 of which were scored at his home ground.
a) Write down the fraction (in its lowest terms) of goals scored at his home ground.
b) Calculate the fraction of goals scored away from home.

Don't forget to make the bottom numbers the same when adding (or subtracting) fractions... It's all a bit of a breeze, really.

Fractions

Q7 A ball is dropped from a height of 6 m.

This stuff is pretty easy — but you don't want to go making silly mistakes in the exam. Get the practice in now.

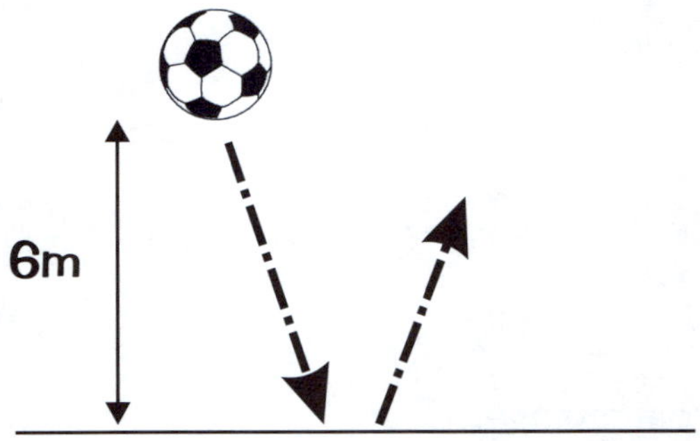

After each bounce the ball rises to $\frac{2}{3}$ of its previous height.
What height will it reach after the third bounce?

Q8 George wants to make a cake. The recipe requires 150 g each of flour, sugar and butter, and 3 eggs. George only has 2 eggs, so he decides to make a smaller cake with the same proportions.

a) How much flour will George need to use?
b) If each egg weighs 25 g, how much will the cake weigh before it goes in the oven?
c) What fraction of the uncooked weight is flour?
d) If the cake loses $\frac{1}{7}$ of its weight during baking (due to moisture loss), what will it weigh after baking?

Q9 The population of Australia is 18 million, of which 3.5 million people live in Sydney and 1 million people live in Perth.
a) What fraction of the population live in Perth?
b) What fraction of the population live in Perth or Sydney?

Q10 Green Island is split into six regions A, B, C, D, E and F. The areas of the six regions are 12, 2, 3, 18, 4 and 9 km^2 respectively.
a) What is the total area of the island?
b) What fraction of the island's area is taken up by the two largest regions?

Q11 In a consumer survey, 100 people stated their favourite vegetable. 25 people chose peas, 35 carrots and 32 runner beans.
a) How many of the 100 people chose a vegetable other than peas, carrots or runner beans?
b) What fraction of the 100 people chose carrots as their favourite vegetable?
c) What fraction of the 100 people chose peas as their favourite vegetable?
d) At least how many people chose a green vegetable as their favourite?
e) Not more than how many people chose a green vegetable as their favourite?

Percentages

Make sure you can switch from fractions to decimals to percentages before you start.

Q1 Express each percentage as a decimal:

a) 50% **b)** 12% **c)** 40% **d)** 34%

Q2 Express each percentage as a fraction in its lowest terms:

a) 25% **b)** 60% **c)** 45% **d)** 30%

Q3 Express each of the following as a percentage:

a) $\frac{1}{8}$ **b)** 0.23 **c)** $\frac{12}{40}$ **d)** 0.34

Q4 In a French test Lauren scored 17/20. What percentage is this?

There are three types of percentage question. The first one is working out "something % of something else" — it's dead easy. Just remember to add it back on to the original amount if you've got a VAT question.

Oh look...

Q5 87 out of 120 pupils at Backwater School have access to a computer. What percentage is this?

Q6

Four friends stay at the Pickled Parrot Hotel for a night and each take an evening meal. Bed and Breakfast costs £37 per person and the evening meal costs £15 per person. How much is the total cost, if VAT is added at $17\frac{1}{2}$%?

Q7 John bought a new video recorder. The tag in the shop said it cost £299 + VAT. If VAT is charged at $17\frac{1}{2}$%, how much did he pay (to the nearest penny)?

Q8 Donald earns an annual wage of £23,500. He doesn't pay tax on the first £3400 that he earns. How much income tax does he pay a year if the rate of tax is:

a) 25%
b) 40%?

Q9 Tanya paid £6500 for her new car. Each year its value decreased by 8%.

a) How much was it worth when it was one year old?
b) How much was it worth when it was two years old?

Here's the 2nd type — finding "something as a percentage of something else" — in this case you're looking at percentage change, so don't forget to work that out first.

Q10 During a rainstorm a water butt increased its weight from 10.4 kg to 13.6 kg. What was the percentage increase (to the nearest per cent)?

Q11 If L = MN, what is the percentage increase in L if M increases by 15% and N increases by 20%?

Percentages

Q12 There are approximately 6000 fish-and-chip shops in the UK. On average, a fish-and-chip shop gets about 160 visitors each day. Given that the population of the UK is roughly 60 million, approximately what percentage of the population visit a fish-and-chip shop each day?

Q13 An electrical store reduces the price of a particular camera from £90.00 to £78.30. What is the percentage reduction (to 1 d.p.)?

Q14 I wish to invest £1000 for a period of three years and have decided to place my money with the Highrise Building Society on 1 January. If I choose to use the Gold Account I will withdraw the interest at the end of each year. If I choose to use the Silver Account I will leave the interest to be added to the capital at the end of each year.

Highrise Building Society

Gold Account	7.875% p.a
Silver Account	7.00% p.a

Interest is calculated day by day and added to your account on 31 December each year

a) Calculate the total interest I will receive if I use the Gold Account.

b) Calculate the total interest I will receive if I use the Silver Account.

After some thought I decide to use the Gold Account and leave the interest to be added to the capital at the end of each year.

c) Calculate the total interest I will now receive from the Gold Account.

Q15 At birth, Veronica was 0.3 m tall. By adulthood she had grown to 1.5 m tall. Calculate her height now as a percentage of her height at birth.

Q16 Jeremy wanted a new sofa for his lounge. A local furniture shop had just what he was looking for — and for only £130.00 + VAT. Jeremy had £150 in his bank account. If VAT was charged at $17\frac{1}{2}$%, could Jeremy afford the sofa?

Q17 Desmond's GCSE maths exam is next week. As part of his revision he attempted 31 questions on his least favourite topic of percentages. He got 21 questions fully right on the first attempt. Two days later he tried all 31 questions again and this time got 29 correct.

a) What percentage of questions did he get correct on his first attempt?
b) What percentage of questions did he get correct on his second attempt?
c) What is the percentage improvement in Desmond's results?

Ooh... here's the 3rd type — finding the original value. The bit most people get wrong is deciding whether the value given represents more or less than 100% of the original — so always check your answer makes sense.

Q18 In the new year sales Robin bought a tennis racket for £68.00. The original price had been reduced by 15%. What was the original price?

Q19 There were 300 people living in a certain village a year ago. Today the population of the village is 360.

a) What is the annual percentage increase in the population?
b) Assuming the percentage increase is constant, how many whole years from today will it be before the population has more than doubled its current size?

Growth and Decay

Hey look — it's another of those "there is only one formula to learn and you use it for every question" topics.

So I reckon you'd better learn The Formula then...

Q1 Calculate the amount in each account if:

a) £200 is invested for 10 years at 9% compound interest per annum
b) £500 is invested for 3 years at 7% compound interest per annum
c) £750 is invested for 30 months at 8% compound interest per annum
d) £1000 is invested for 15 months at 6.5% compound interest per annum.

Q2 A colony of bacteria grows at the compound rate of 12% per hour. Initially there are 200 bacteria.

a) How many will there be after 3 hours?
b) How many will there be after 1 day?
c) After how many whole hours will there be at least 4000 bacteria? (solve this by trial and error)

Q3 A radioactive element was observed every day and the mass remaining was measured. Initially there was 9 kg but this decreased at the compound rate of 3% per day. How much radioactive element will be left after:

a) 3 days **b)** 6 days **c)** 1 week **d)** 4 weeks?
Give your answer to no more than 3 d.p.

Q4 The population of a country is 16 million, and the annual compound growth rate is estimated to be 1.3%. Predict the country's population in:

a) 4 years' time **b)** 20 years' time.

Q5 Mrs Smith decides to invest £7000 in a savings account. She has the choice of putting all her money into an account paying 5% compound interest per annum, or she can put half of her investment into an instant account paying 6% compound interest per annum and the remaining half into an instant access account paying 4% per annum. If she left the investment alone for 3 years, which is her best option and by how much?

Q6 Money is invested on the stock market. During a recession the value of the shares fall by 2% per week. Find the value of the stock if:

a) £2000 was invested for a fortnight
b) £30,000 was invested for 4 weeks
c) £500 was invested for 7 weeks
d) £100,000 was invested for a year.

Q7 A car is estimated to depreciate in value by 14% each year. Find the estimated values of these used cars:

a) a Peugeot 206 which cost £8,495 six months ago
b) a BMW which cost £34,000 eighteen months ago
c) a Volvo S40 which cost £13,495 two years ago
d) a Vauxhall Vectra which cost £14,395 two years ago
e) a Ford Escort which cost £11,295 three years ago
f) a Daewoo Nexia which cost £6,795 twelve months ago.

Ratios

I don't want to spoil the surprise, but you're going to need your calculator for this bit — get your finger on that fraction button...

RATIOS are like FRACTIONS which are like DECIMALS

We can treat the RATIO 3:4 like the FRACTION $\frac{3}{4}$, which is 0.75 as a DECIMAL.

Watch out though — this isn't $\frac{3}{4}$ of the total:
If there are girls and boys in the ratio 3:4, it means there's $\frac{3}{4}$ as many girls as boys.
So if there's 8 boys, there's $\frac{3}{4} \times 8 = 6$ girls.

Q1 Write these ratios in their simplest forms:

a) 6 : 8 **c)** 1.5 : 3 **e)** 2 weeks : 4 days
b) 5 : 20 **d)** $2\frac{1}{4}$: 4 **f)** £1.26 : 14p

Q2 A rectangle has sides in the ratio 1:2. Calculate the length of the longer side if the shorter side is:

a) 3 cm **b)** 5.5 cm **c)** 15.2 m

Calculate the length of the shorter side if the longer side is:

d) 3 cm **e)** 5.5 cm **f)** 15.2 m

Q3 Divide the following amounts in the ratios given:

a) £20 in the ratio 2 : 3 **c)** 500 g in the ratio 1 : 2 : 2
b) 150 m in the ratio 8 : 7 **d)** 8 hrs in the ratio 1 : 2 : 3

For questions like this, add up the ratio numbers to find the total number of parts and divide by this. Then multiply by each number in the ratio separately to find the different amounts.

Q4 **a)** Increase £3.20 in the ratio 2 : 3.
b) Decrease 120 cm in the ratio 3 : 2.

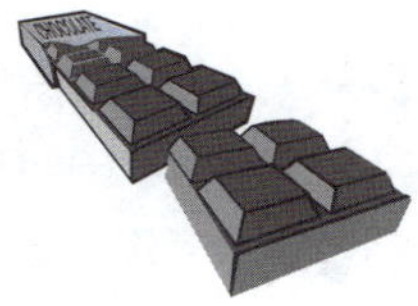

Q5 John and Peter share a bar of chocolate marked into 16 squares. They share it in the ratio 1 : 3. How many squares does each boy get?

Q6

A 2 litre bottle of cola is to be shared between three girls in the ratio 2 : 3 : 5. How many millilitres will each girl get?

Watch out for your units — you'll have to change them over for this one — and your answer should be in millilitres.

Q7 Oak and ash saplings are planted along a roadside in the ratio 2 : 3 respectively. If there are 20 oak saplings, how many ash saplings are there?

Q8 Tony gives £100 to be shared by Jane, Paul and Rosemary in ratio according to their age. Jane is 10, Paul is 12 and Rosemary is 3 years old. How much will each child get?

Calculator Buttons

Q1 Using the x^2 button on your calculator, work out:

a) 1^2 **b)** 2^2 **c)** 11^2
d) 16^2 **e)** $(-1)^2$ **f)** 30^2
g) $(-5)^2$ **h)** 1000^2 **i)** 0^2

(For parts **e)** and **g)** use your (−) button)

Q2 Using the √ button on your calculator, work out:

a) $\sqrt{16}$ **b)** $\sqrt{36}$ **c)** $\sqrt{289}$
d) $\sqrt{0}$ **e)** $\sqrt{3600}$ **f)** $\sqrt{400}$
g) $\sqrt{3}$ **h)** $\sqrt{7}$ **i)** $\sqrt{30}$

Q3 For his birthday Lars Larson was given a new calculator. He pressed the button 2 and then he pressed x^2 and then =. He then pressed the Ans button and the x^2 button, then the = button 8 more times. Much to Lars' alarm, a message appeared in the display. What was the message and why did it appear?

Q4 Use the ∛ button on your calculator to work out:

a) $\sqrt[3]{1}$ **b)** $\sqrt[3]{0}$ **c)** $\sqrt[3]{343}$ **d)** $\sqrt[3]{1000}$
e) $\sqrt[3]{27}$ **f)** $\sqrt[3]{-27}$ **g)** $\sqrt[3]{-64}$ **h)** $\sqrt[3]{-5}$

Yeah, OK, we all know how to do sums on a calculator — but it can do so much more... check out the groovy powers button and the funky brackets buttons, not to mention the slinky 1/x button...

Q5 By calculating the bottom line first (the denominator) and then using your calculator's memory buttons, work out:

a) $\frac{21}{2 + \sin 30°}$ **b)** $\frac{\tan 15°}{12 + 12^2}$
c) $\frac{15}{\cos 30° + 22}$ **d)** $\frac{18}{3 + \sqrt[3]{12}}$
e) $\frac{12}{12 + \tan 60°}$ **f)** $\frac{18}{11 + \tan 77°}$

Q6 Using (and) calculate:

Here comes BODMAS...

a) $\frac{(14 + 18)}{(2 \times 8)}$ **b)** $\frac{8}{(1 \times 4)(8 - 6)}$
c) $\frac{(9 + (4 \div 2))}{(11 \times 3)}$ **d)** $\frac{14(4 \times 8)}{(6 + 9)}$
e) $\frac{12}{(8 + 9)(13 - 11)}$ **f)** $\frac{7(5 + 4)}{12(9 \times 8)}$

Calculator Buttons

Q7 Using the **x^y** button, find:

a) 2^0 **b)** 4^{10} **c)** 2^{20} **d)** π^2 **e)** 14^3 **f)** 3^{10} **g)** $(\cos 30°)^5$ **h)** 4.29^7 **i)** $(\sin 45°)^4$

Q8 Using the **EXP** or **EE** button on your calculator, enter the following numbers into your calculator and write down what you get:

a) 2×10^4
b) 3×10^5
c) 6.29×10^4

Remember — when you use the standard form button, your calculator gives you the answer as 2.3^{43}, when it <u>really</u> means 2.3×10^{43}. It's up to you to write it in the correct form, or <u>your answer will be wrong</u>.

Q9 Work out (leaving your answer in standard form):

a) $\frac{2 \times 10^3}{5 \times 10^2}$ **b)** $\frac{5.6 \times 10^4}{2.8 \times 10^5}$ **c)** $\frac{1.88 \times 10^3}{9.4 \times 10^2}$ **d)** $\frac{4.2 \times 10^9}{3.9 \times 10^2}$ **e)** $\frac{7.1 \times 10^3}{3.52 \times 10^3}$ **f)** $(8.92 \times 10^6) \times (1.22 \times 10^2)$

Number Crossword

ACROSS

1) An imperial length. (4)
5) π is not this kind of number. (8)
7) Centre pages (anag)? (11)
9) The __________ of 24 are 1, 2, 3, 4, 6, 12 and 24. (7)

DOWN

2) 2 points in a game of rugby, but these are also required to find the equivalent reading of Celsius from Fahrenheit, hours from minutes, for example. (10)
3) I am divisible only by myself and one. (5)
4) You may add and subtract these where they share a common denominator. (9)
6) A guess based on deduction. (8)
8) I'm irrational but not absurd. (5)

Conversion Factors

Q1 Convert the following into just hours:

a) 2 hours and 20 minutes **b)** 3 hours and 6 minutes **c)** 20 minutes.

Q2 The times below are taken from a 12-hour clock. Give the equivalent 24-hour readings.

a) 11.30 pm
b) 10.22 am
c) 12.15 am
d) 12.15 pm
e) 8.30 am
f) 4.45 pm

Q3 The Bon Voyage Holiday Company are offering an exchange rate of 1.48 euros for £1 sterling. They are also offering 11.03 Danish kroner for £1 sterling and 2.45 Australian dollars for £1 sterling. Calculate, to the nearest penny, the sterling equivalent of:

a) 220 euros
b) 686 Danish kroner
c) 1664 Australian dollars
d) 148 euros
e) 15 Danish kroner
f) 1950 Australian dollars
g) 899 Danish kroner
h) 20 euros
i) 668 Australian dollars
j) 3389 Danish kroner
k) 1000 Australian dollars
l) 1 euro

Q4 Convert the following into hours and minutes:

a) 3.25 hours **b)** 0.4 hours **c)** 7.3 hours **d)** 1.2 hours.

Q5 The scale on a map is 1:10,000.
How big are the following in real life:

a) a distance of 2 cm on the map
b) a distance of 20 cm on the map
c) a distance of 70 cm on the map
d) an area of 2 cm^2 on the map?

Maps can be tricky, the best thing is to convert the numbers you're given to life-size distances, then do another conversion to the appropriate units.

Q6 Another map has a scale of 1:3000.
What size on this map are the following:

a) a distance of 5 km in real life
b) a distance of 1 km in real life
c) an area of 100 m^2 in real life
d) an area of 50 m^2 in real life?

Just remember — the distance on the map is unlikely to be larger than the real-life distance.

Metric and Imperial Units

You've got to know all the metric and imperial conversion factors. There's no way out of it — you'll just have to sit down and learn them. Sorry and all that...

Q1 Express the given quantities in terms of the unit(s) in brackets:

a) 2 m [cm]	**g)** 87 in [ft and in]	**m)** 6 ft [in]	**s)** 8 cm 6 mm [mm]
b) 3.3 cm [mm]	**h)** 43 oz [lb and oz]	**n)** 5 lb [oz]	**t)** 3 ft 6 in [in]
c) 4 kg [g]	**i)** 650 m [km]	**o)** 301 ft [yd and ft]	**u)** 4 lb 7 oz [oz]
d) 600 g [kg]	**j)** 9 kg [g]	**p)** 6 m [mm]	**v)** 550 kg [t]
e) 4 ft [in]	**k)** 7 g [kg]	**q)** 2 t [kg]	**w)** 3 m 54 cm [cm]
f) 36 in [ft]	**l)** 950 g [kg]	**r)** 3000 g [kg]	**x)** 0.7cm [mm]

Q2 Deborah weighs 9 stone 4 pounds.
There are 14 pounds in a stone and 1 kilogram is equal to 0.157 stone.
Change Deborah's weight into kilograms.

Q3 A horse's drinking trough holds 14 gallons of water.
Approximately how many litres is this?

Q4 Convert 147 g into ounces.

Q5 Barbara cycled 51 km in one day, while Barry cycled 30 miles. Who cycled further?

Q6 A pile of bricks weighs 7 metric tonnes. How many imperial tons is this?

Q7 A seamstress needs to cut an 11-inch strip of finest Chinese silk.
a) How many cm is this?
b) How many mm is this?

Q8 At the gym Arnold can lift a barbell weighing 60 kg.
a) Approximately how many lb can Arnold lift?
b) How many ounces is this?
Sylvester can lift a barbell weighing 0.059 tonnes.
c) Who can lift the most?

Q9 A recipe for The World's Wobbliest Jelly requires 5 lb of sugar. How many 1 kg bags of sugar does Dick need to buy so that he can make a jelly?

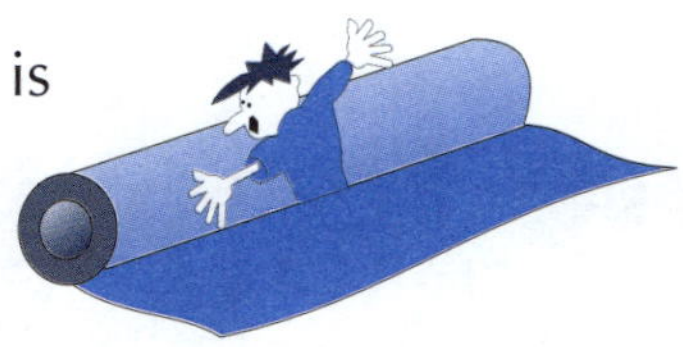

Q10 Neil is going to buy some fabric for a new pair of trousers that he is going to make. A local shop prices the fabric that he would like at £9.84 per square yard. A fabric superstore prices the same fabric at £10.80 per square metre. According to price, where should Neil buy his fabric? (Use the conversion factor 91 cm = 1 yard.)

Q11 The priceless Greek statue in my garden is 21 feet tall.
a) How many inches is this?
b) How many yards is this?
c) How many metres is this?
d) How many cm is this?
e) How many mm is this?
f) How many km is this?

Q12

1 pint=0.568 litres
£1=$1.42

Which is better value, 2 pints of beer for $5.76 or 1 litre of beer for £3.92?

Estimating

Q1 Without using your calculator, find approximate answers to the following:

a) 6560×1.97
b) 8091×1.456
c) $38.45 \times 1.4237 \times 5.0002$
d) $45.34 \div 9.345$
e) $34504 \div 7133$
f) $\frac{55.33 \times 19.345}{9.23}$

g) 7139×2.13
h) $98 \times 2.54 \times 2.033$
i) $21 \times 21 \times 21$
j) $8143 \div 81$
k) $62000 \div 950$
l) $\pi \div 3$

Always give your answer to one less significant figure than the question.

Q2 Estimate the area under the graph.

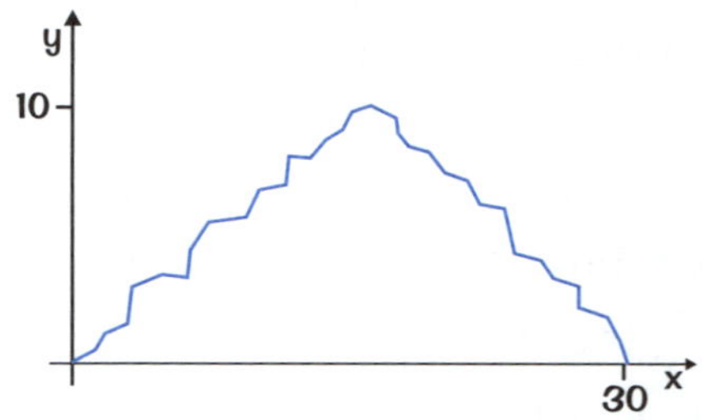

Q3 A supermarket chain sold 14634 tins of beans during a four-week period.
a) If the supermarkets were open every day of the week, how many days did it take to sell the 14 634 tins of beans?
b) What was the average amount of beans sold each day?
c) Show your working for a rough estimate to **b)** to check that your answer is of the right order of magnitude. ***"Of the right order of magnitude" just means "the right size", by the way.***

Q4 Showing all your working, estimate the following:

a) $\frac{144.5 + 49.1}{153.2 - 41.2}$

b) $\frac{18.2 \times 10.7}{\sqrt{398.6}}$

c) $\frac{2021.23 \times 4.0436}{20.33 \times 4.902}$

d) $\frac{(9.2)^2 \div 10.3}{4.306 \times 5.011}$

If you don't show your working you'll lose easy marks, so it's gotta be worth doing.

Q5 Estimate these volumes:

a)

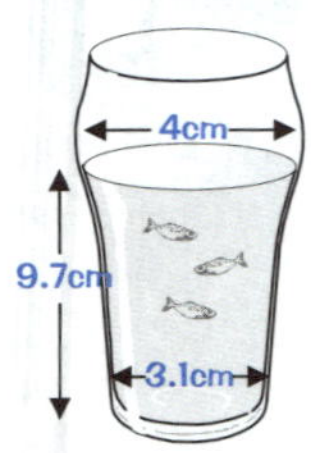

b)

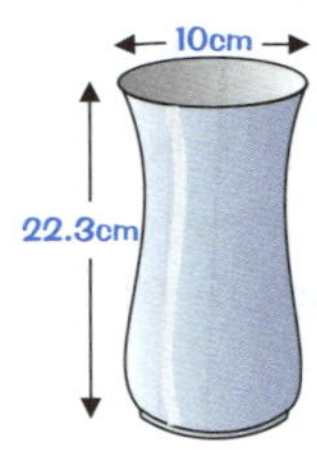

Q6 Here is a sequence of square numbers. Use it to estimate (to 1 d.p.) the square roots below.

12	**13**	**14**	**15**	**16**	**17**	**18**	**19**	**20**
144	**169**	**196**	**225**	**256**	**289**	**324**	**361**	**400**

a) $\sqrt{405}$ **b)** $\sqrt{270}$ **c)** $\sqrt{250}$ **d)** $\sqrt{375}$ **e)** $\sqrt{391}$

Rounding Off

Rounding a number off to a certain number of decimal places or significant figures is really quite easy — the tricky bit's when they ask for minimum and maximum values...

Q1 K = 456.9873
Write K correct to:

a) three significant figures
b) two significant figures
c) one significant figure.

Q2 John divides £14.30 by 3. What is the answer correct to the nearest penny?

Q3 Calculate, giving your answers to a sensible degree of accuracy:

a) $\frac{42.65 \times 0.9863}{24.6 \times 2.43}$

b) $\frac{13.63 + 7.22}{13.63 - 7.22}$

Remember — the real value could be anything up to half a unit above or below the rounded off value.

Q4 Sandra has a parcel to post. To find out how much it will cost she weighs it.
a) A set of kitchen scales, that weigh to the nearest 10 g, show that the parcel weighs 90 g. Write down the upper bound of the weight of the parcel.
b) Next she weighs the parcel on a different set of kitchen scales, which are accurate to the nearest 5 g. The packet weighs 95 g. Write down the upper and lower bounds of the weight of the package according to these scales.
c) The post office weighs the parcel on some electronic scales to the nearest gram. It weighs 98 g. Can all the scales be right?

Q5 a) The length of a rectangle is measured as 12 ± 0.1 cm. The width of the same rectangle is measured as 4 ± 0.1 cm. Calculate the perimeter of the rectangle, giving also the maximum possible error.
b) A rectangle measures A ± x cm in length and B ± y cm in width. The formula P = 2(A + B) is used to calculate the perimeter, P, of the rectangle. What is the maximum possible error in P?

Q6 Calculate, giving your answers to a sensible degree of accuracy:

a) $\frac{18.95 \times 0.6464}{2.4 - 2.0}$ **b)** $\frac{324 + 7.22}{243 - 7.2}$

Q7 Jodie weighs herself on some scales that are accurate to the nearest 10 grams. The digital display shows her weight as 64.78 kg.
a) What is the maximum that she could weigh?
b) What is the minimum that she could weigh?

Upper/lower bounds are just another way of saying the maximum/minimum possible values.

Q8 A = 13, correct to 2 significant figures.
B = 12.5, correct to 3 significant figures.
a) For the value of A, write down the upper bound and the lower bound.
b) For the value of B, write down the upper bound and the lower bound.
c) Calculate the upper bound and lower bound for C when C = AB.

Direct and Inverse Proportion

Q1 If 17 textbooks cost £150.45, how much will 28 cost?

Q2 If it takes 4 people 28 hours to complete a task, how long would it take just one person?

Q3 A person earns £6.20 an hour. How much do they earn for $15\frac{1}{2}$ hours' work?

Q4 On a map 2 cm represents 3 km.

a) Two towns are 14 km apart. What is the distance between them on the map?

b) Two road junctions are 20.3 cm apart on the map. What is their real distance apart?

Q5 y is directly proportional to x. If $y = 5$ when x is 25, find y when x is 100.

Q6 y is directly proportional to x. If y is 1.2 when x is 2.5, find the value of y when $x = 3.75$.

Q7 If $y \propto x$ and $y = 132$ when $x = 10$, find the value of y when $x = 14$.

Q8 If $y \propto x$ and $y = 117$ when $x = 45$, find the value of x when $y = 195$.

Q9 Complete the following tables of values where y is always directly proportional to x:

a)

x	2	4	6
y	5	10	

b)

x	3	6	9
y		9	

c)

x	27		
y	5	10	15

Q10 If $y = 3$ when $x = 8$ and y is inversely proportional to x, find the value of y when $x = 12$.

Q11 If $y \propto \frac{1}{x}$ and $x = 4$ when $y = 5$, find the value of x when $y = 10$.

Q12 If y and x vary inversely and $y = 12$ when $x = 3$, find:

a) the value of x when $y = 9$

b) the value of y when $x = 6$.

Q13 A man travels for 2 hours at 72 km per hour, completing a journey between two towns. Meanwhile another man completes the same journey at a speed of 80 km per hour. How long did it take him?

Q14 Given that $y \propto \frac{1}{x}$, complete this table of values.

x	1	2	3	4	5	6
y					9.6	

Make sure you know ALL the details about Direct and Inverse Proportion.

Direct & Inverse Proportion

Q15 The area of a circle is proportional to the square of the radius. If the area is 113 cm^2 when the radius is 6 cm, find:

a) the area of a circle with radius 5 cm

b) the radius of a circle with area 29 cm^2.

Give your answers to 1 d.p.

Q16 y is inversely proportional to the square of x, and $y = 4$ when $x = 6$. Find the value of:

a) y when $x = 3$

b) x when $y = 9$, given that x is negative.

Q17 If $y \propto x^2$ and $y = 4$ when $x = 4$, find the value of y when $x = 12$.

Q18 $y = kx^3$ and $y = 200$ when $x = 5$.

a) Find the value of k.

b) Find the value of y when $x = 8$.

c) Find the value of x when $y = 2433.4$.

Q19 Given that y varies inversely as the square of x, complete the following tables of values, given that x is always positive.

x	1	2	5	
y			4	1

x	2			8
y	24	6	$2\frac{2}{3}$	

Q20 Two cylindrical containers are filled to the same depth, d cm, with water. The mass of the water in each container is proportional to the square of the radius of each container. The first container has a radius of 16 cm and the water has a mass of 16 kg. If the second container has a radius of 8 cm, find the mass of the water inside it.

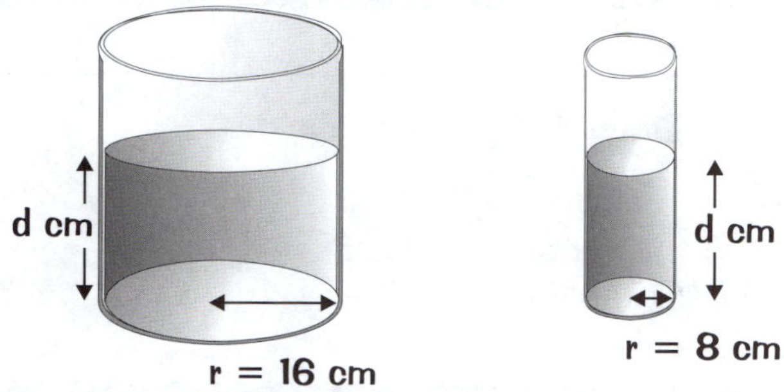

Q21 Given that r varies inversely as the square of s, and $r = 24$ when $s = 10$, find the values of:

a) r when $s = 5$.

b) s when $r = 150$, given that s is positive.

c) r when $s = 2$.

d) s when $r = 37\frac{1}{2}$, given that s is negative.

Don't forget about that little joker, the "inverse square" variation — they'll expect you to know that, too.

Q22 The table shows how y varies with x.

a) Write down the equation which shows how y varies with x.

b) Find the value of y when $x = 6.4$.

c) Find the value of x when $y = 16$.

x	1.2	2.5	3.2	4.8
y	$166\frac{2}{3}$	80	62.5	$41\frac{2}{3}$

Plotting Curves

In case you hadn't noticed, it's always a good idea to put lots of steps in the table of values — that way it's easier to check any points that look wrong.

Q1 Complete this table of values for $y = x^2 + 2$:

x	-3	-2	-1	0	1	2	3
x^2							
+2							
y							

Draw the graph of $y = x^2 + 2$.

Q2 Complete this table of values for $y = 2x^2 - 4$:

x	-3	-2	-1	0	1	2	3
$2x^2$							
-4							
y							

Draw the graph of $y = 2x^2 - 4$.

Q3 Complete this table of values for $y = -x^2 + 2$:

x	-3	-2	-1	0	1	2	3
$-x^2$							
+2							
y							

Draw the graph of $y = -x^2 + 2$.

Q4 Complete this table of values for $y = -2x^2 + 6$:

x	-3	-2	-1	0	1	2	3
$-2x^2$							
+6							
y							

Draw the graph of $y = -2x^2 + 6$.

Q5 Complete this table of values for $y = x^3$:

x	-3	-2	-1	0	1	2	3
$y=x^3$							

Draw the graph of $y = x^3$.

Q6 Complete this table of values for $y = -x^3$:

x	-3	-2	-1	0	1	2	3
$y=-x^3$							

Draw the graph of $y = -x^3$.

Q7 Complete this table of values for $y = x^3 + 4$:

x	-3	-2	-1	0	1	2	3
x^3							
+4							
Y							

Draw the graph of $y = x^3 + 4$.

Q8 Complete this table of values for $y = -x^3 - 4$:

x	-3	-2	-1	0	1	2	3
$-x^3$							
-4							
y							

Draw the graph of $y = -x^3 - 4$.

Q9 Look at your graphs for Questions 5 and 7. What has been done to Graph 5 to change it into Graph 7? Without plotting a table of values, draw the graph of $y = x^3 - 4$.

Q10 Look at your graphs for Questions 6 and 8. What has been done to Graph 6 to change it into Graph 8? Without plotting a table of values, draw the graph of $y = -x^3 + 4$.

Plotting Straight-Line Graphs

Q1 Complete the following table for the line $y = 3x - 1$:

x	-4	-3	-2	-1	0	1	2	3	4
3x									
-1									
y									

Plot these points on graph paper and hence draw the graph of $y = 3x - 1$. Use a scale of 1 cm for 2 units on the y-axis and 2 cm for 1 unit on the x-axis.

Q2 Complete the following table for the line $y = 2x - 2$:

x	-4	-3	-2	-1	0	1	2	3	4
2x									
-2									
y									

Plot these points on graph paper and hence draw the graph of $y = 2x - 2$.

Q3 Complete the following table for the line $y = \frac{1}{2}x - 3$:

x	-6	-4	-2	0	2	4	6
½ x							
-3							
y							

Plot these points on graph paper and hence draw the graph of $y = \frac{1}{2}x - 3$.

Q4 Complete the following table for the line $y = \frac{1}{4}x - 4$:

x	-8	-4	0	4	8	12	16
¼ x							
-4							
y							

Plot these points on graph paper and hence draw the graph of $y = \frac{1}{4}x - 4$.

To plot a straight line, the *very first thing* you've got to do is work out a *table of values*, then once you know they're in a straight line, just get your ruler out and you're away.

Plotting Straight-Line Graphs

Q5 Complete this table of values for $y = \frac{1}{4}x - 3$:

x	-8	-4	8
y			

Plot these points on graph paper and draw the graph of $y = \frac{1}{4}x - 3$.
Use your graph to find:

a) The value of y when $x = 2$
b) The value of y when $x = 0$
c) The value of x when $y = -2$
d) The value of x when $y = -1.5$

Q6 Complete the following table for the line $y = -2x + 4$:

x	-4	0	4
y			

Plot these points on graph paper and draw the graph of $y = -2x + 4$.
Use your graph to find:

a) The value of y when $x = 3$
b) The value of y when $x = -1$
c) The value of x when $y = 10$
d) The value of x when $y = -2$

Q7 Complete the following table for the line $y = -x + 3$:

x	-4	2	6
y			

Plot these points on graph paper and draw the graph of $y = -x + 3$.
Use your graph to find:

a) The value of y when $x = 4$
b) The value of y when $x = 1$
c) The value of x when $y = 2$
d) The value of x when $y = 5$

Q8 Complete the following table for the line $y = -\frac{x}{4} - 2$:

x	-12	-6	6
y			

Plot these points on graph paper and draw the graph of $y = -\frac{x}{4} - 2$.
Use your graph to find:

a) The value of y when $x = -4$
b) The value of y when $x = -1$
c) The value of x when $y = -2.75$
d) The value of x when $y = 0$

Q9 The cost of hiring a car is calculated using the formula:
Total cost = £25 + 20p for each kilometre travelled.
Copy and complete this table:

Number of kilometres	0	50	100	200	300	350
Total cost in £						

Plot these points on a graph (put distance travelled on the horizontal axis and total cost on the vertical axis).

Use your graph to find the cost of hiring the car when the following distances have been travelled:

a) 170 km
b) 270 km
c) 320 km.

Use your graph to find the number of kilometres travelled when this total cost is:

d) £78
e) £34
f) £42.

Solving Equations Using Graphs

This is a nice easy way of solving simultaneous equations. All you've got to do is draw 2 straight-line graphs and read off a value where they cross each other. It does mean you've got to be up to speed with your straight-line graphs, though...

Q1 The simultaneous equations given below have been plotted as straight-line graphs. Write down the solutions of the simultaneous equations by looking at the graphs. Finally check your answers by substituting them back into the simultaneous equations.

a) $y + 2x = 9$
$3y = x + 6$

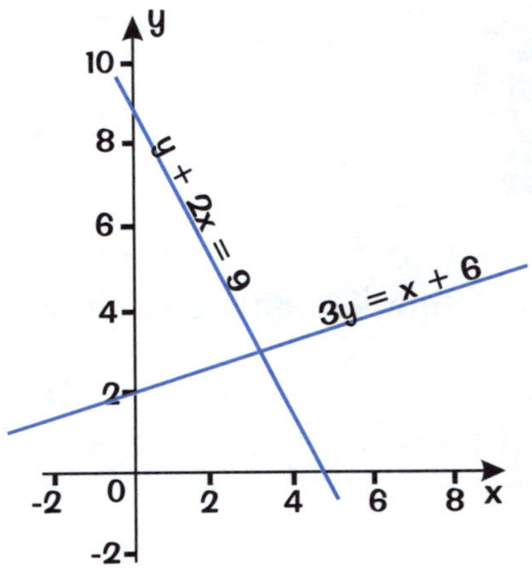

b) $y = 2x - 13$
$2y + x + 6 = 0$

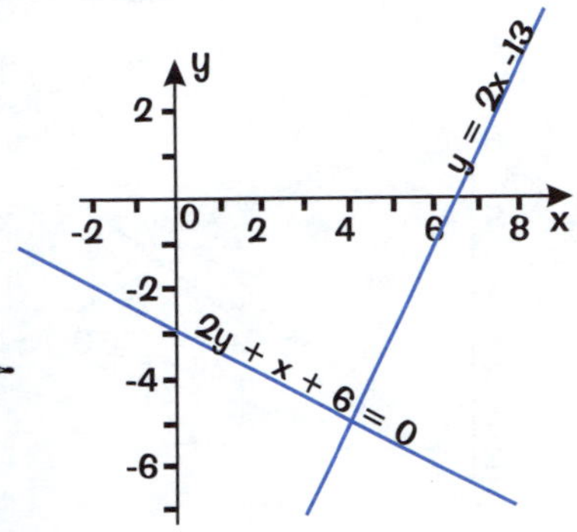

c) $y + x = 1$
$3y = x + 11$

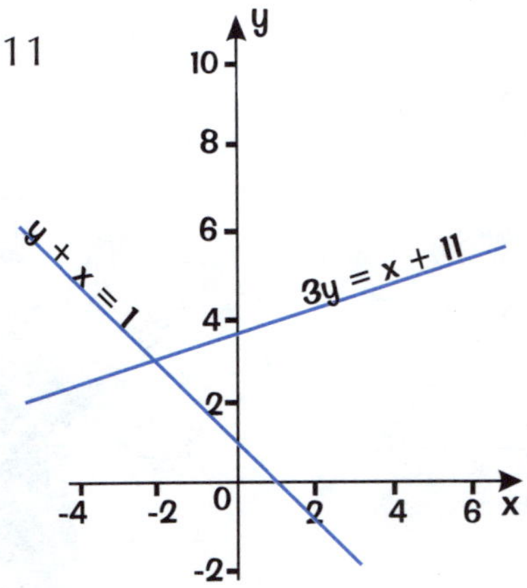

d) $2y = 8 - x$
$2y = x - 2$

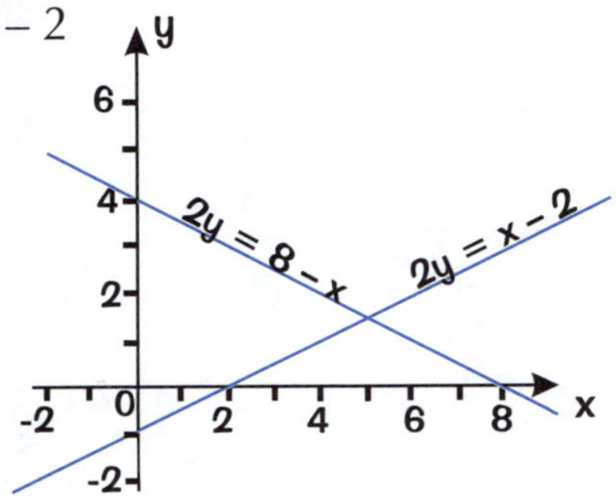

Q2 For each pair of simultaneous equations below:

i) draw and label a pair of axes with x from –3 to 7, and y from –6 to 6

ii) complete two tables of values

iii) plot two straight-line graphs onto your axes, remembering to label each graph

iv) use your graphs to find the values of x and y that satisfy both equations

v) check your answers by substituting them into both of the equations.

a) $y = x + 2$
$y = 3x - 2$

b) $y = 2x - 2$
$2y = x + 8$

c) $y = x + 1$
$y = 2x - 2$

d) $y = x + 3$
$y = 3x - 1$

e) $y = 2x + 3$
$y = x - 1$

f) $y = 2 - x$
$y = \frac{1}{2}x - 1$

g) $y = x - 1$
$2y = x + 1$

h) $y + 2 = 4x$
$y + x = 3$

i) $y + 2 = x$
$y = \frac{1}{2}x + 1$

Solving Equations Using Graphs

Q3 Use the graph to solve the following simultaneous equations:

a) $y - 3x = -7$ and $y + x = 9$
b) $y - 3x = -7$ and $3y - x = 3$
c) $y + x = 9$ and $3y - x = 3$

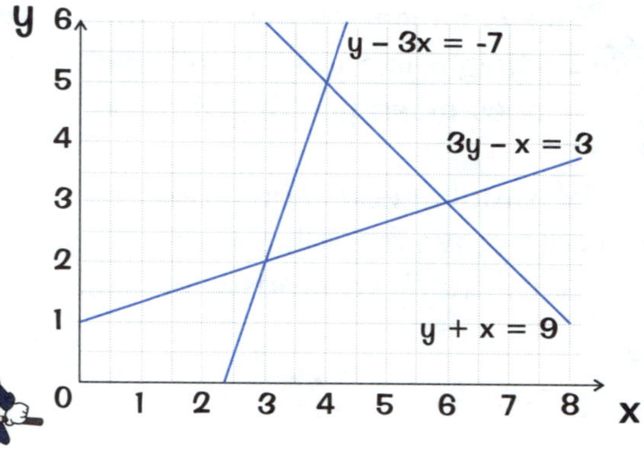

All you've got to be able to do is draw two straight-line graphs and read off a value where they *cross each other*.

Q4

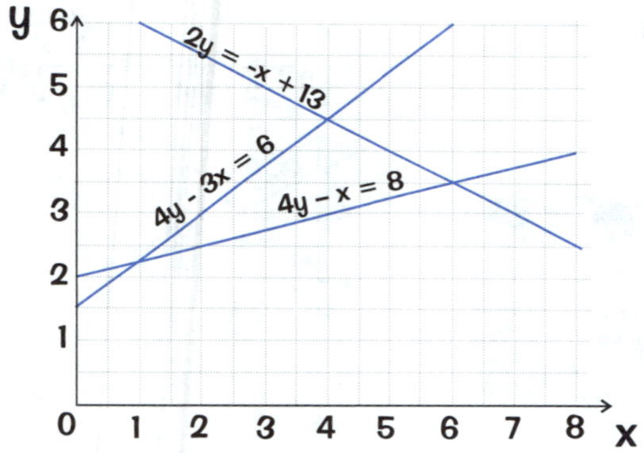

Use the graph to solve the following simultaneous equations:

a) $4y - x = 8$ and $4y - 3x = 6$
b) $4y - x = 8$ and $2y = -x + 13$

Q5 Use the graph to solve the following simultaneous equations:

a) $2y - x = 2$
$y + x = 4$
b) $2y - x = 2$
$2y + x = -6$

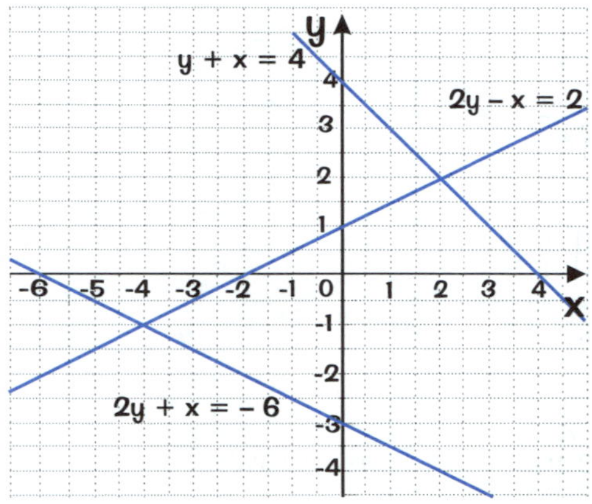

Q6 Solve the following simultaneous equations by drawing graphs. Use values $0 \leqslant x \leqslant 6$.

a) $y = x$
$y = 9 - 2x$
b) $y = 2x + 1$
$2y = 8 + x$
c) $y = 4 - 2x$
$x + y = 3$
d) $y = 3 - x$
$3x + y = 5$
e) $2x + y = 6$
$y = 3x + 1$
f) $y = 2x$
$y = x + 1$
g) $x + y = 5$
$2x - 1 = y$
h) $2y = 3x$
$y = x + 1$
i) $y = x - 3$
$y + x = 7$
j) $y = x + 1$
$2x + y = 10$

Solving Equations Using Graphs

Q7 The diagram shows the graphs:

$y = x^2 - x$
$y = x + 2$
$y = 8$
$y = -2x + 4$

Use the graphs to find the solutions to:

a) $x^2 - x = 0$
b) $x^2 - x = x + 2$
c) $x^2 - x = 8$
d) $x^2 - x = -2x + 4$

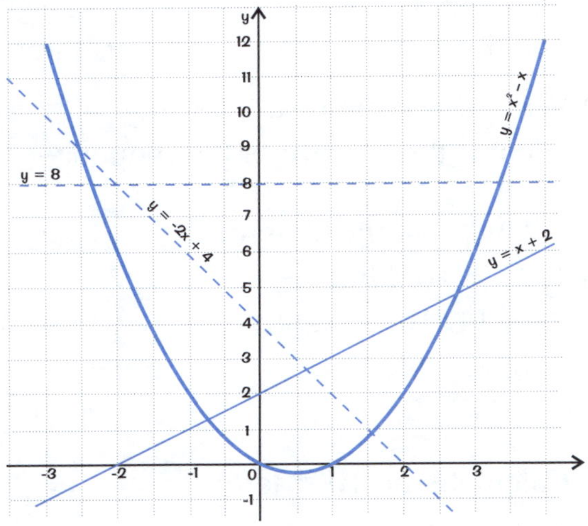

Q8 Complete this table for $y = x^2 - 4$:

x	-4	-3	-2	-1	0	1	2	3	4
x^2									
-4									
y									

Draw the graph of $y = x^2 - 4$.
Use your graph to solve the following equations (to 1 d.p.):

a) $x^2 - 4 = 1$
b) $x^2 - 4 = 0$
c) $x^2 - 4 = x$

Q9 Use graphical methods to solve the following equations:

a) $x^2 + 3x = -2$ (use values $-4 \leqslant x \leqslant 2$)
b) $2x^2 + 5x = -2$ (use values $-3 \leqslant x \leqslant 0$)
c) $x^2 + 3x = x + 4$ (use values $-4 \leqslant x \leqslant 4$)

Q10 An object starts from a point O and moves in a straight line so that at time t seconds its displacement from O is d metres. Its equation is given by $d = \frac{1}{2}t\,(5 - t)$.

a) Complete the following table:

t	0	1	2	2.5	3	4	5	6
½ t								
(5 - t)								
d = ½ t (5 – t)								

b) Draw a graph to show values for t from 0 to 6 on the horizontal scale using a scale of 2 cm to 1 second. Use a scale of 2 cm to 1 metre for values of d on the vertical scale.

c) Use your graph to answer the following questions:
i) After how many seconds does the object return to O?
ii) What was its greatest distance from O during the 6 seconds?
iii) After how many seconds was the object at its greatest distance from O?
iv) After how many seconds was the object 1 metre from O? (give your answer to 1 d.p.)

Sequences

Q1 The first four terms of a sequence are: $1, -\frac{1}{2}, \frac{1}{4}, -\frac{1}{8}$

a) Write down the next 3 terms.

b) What is the nth term of the sequence?

Q2 Write down the nth term:

a) 1, 4, 9, 16, 25...

b) 3, 6, 11, 18, 27...

c) 1, 8, 27, 64, 125...

d) $\frac{1}{2}, 1, 1\frac{1}{2}, 2, 2\frac{1}{2}$...

Q3 Calculate the 100th term:

a) 1, 4, 9, 16 ...

b) $1, \sqrt{2}, \sqrt{3}, \sqrt{4}$ ...

c) $\sqrt{3}, 2, \sqrt{5}, \sqrt{6}$ ...

d) $\sqrt{2}, \sqrt{4}, \sqrt{6}, \sqrt{8}, \sqrt{10}$ ...

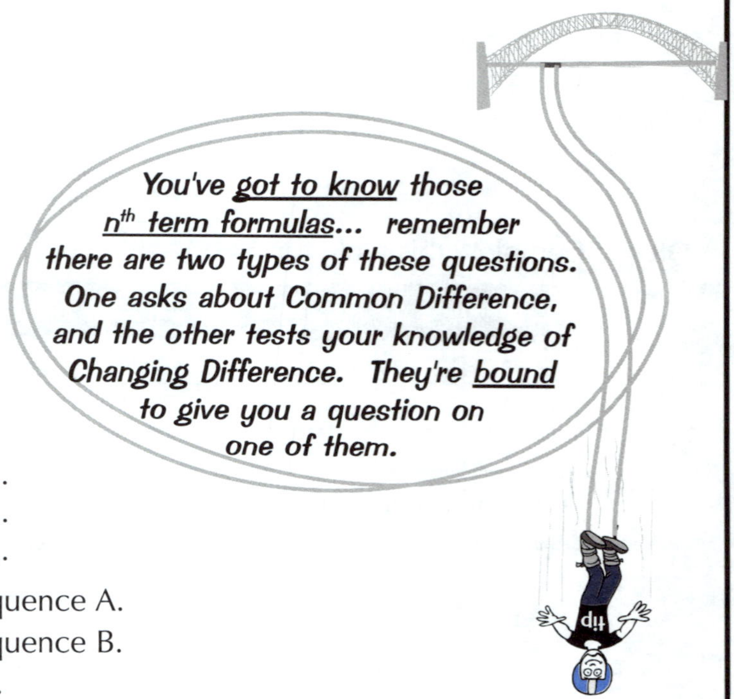

Q4

Sequence A	1, 4, 9, 16, 25,...
Sequence B	3, 6, 9, 12, 15,...
Sequence C	2, 5, 9, 14, 20,...

a) Write down the next three terms in sequence A.

b) Write down the next three terms in sequence B.

c) Write down the nth term of sequence A.

d) Write down the nth term of sequence B.

e) Sequence C is obtained from sequences A and B. Using this information and your answers to parts **c)** and **d)** work out the nth term for sequence C.

f) Calculate the 80th term of sequence C.

Q5 Jimmy uses some stones to make a pattern, as shown.

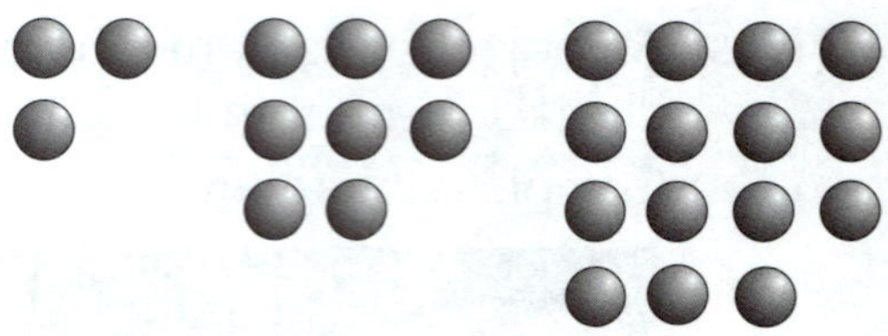

a) How many stones will there be in the next block?

b) How many stones will there be in the nth block?

c) There are 2600 stones in a block. Use your answer to **b)** to find the corresponding value for n.

Q6 The first term of a certain sequence is 1. The second term of the sequence is also 1. The nth term is found using the following formula:

n^{th} term = $(n - 1)^{th}$ term + $(n - 2)^{th}$ term.

Calculate the third, fourth and fifth terms in the sequence.

Q7 In order to work out the evaporation rate, Joanna measured the area of a puddle of water every hour on the hour. At 1300h the area of the puddle was 128 cm^2. 1 hour later the area of the puddle was 64 cm^2. At 1500h the area was 32 cm^2.

a) What was the area of the puddle of water at 1600h?

b) What was the area of the puddle at 1800h?

Sequences

Q8 Write down the next three terms of these sequences:

a) 5, 8, 12, 17,...
b) 6, 9, 14, 21,...
c) 9, 12, 19, 30,...
d) 14, 19, 27, 38,...

If the difference between terms is always decreasing, there's going to be a limit to the sequence.

Q9 The first four terms of a sequence are x, $4x$, $9x$, $16x$.

a) For $x = 2$ write down the next two terms in the sequence.
b) For $x = 2$ write down the nth term in the sequence.
c) For $x = 3$ write down the nth term in the sequence.
d) Write down the nth term, valid for any value of x.
e) For $x = ½$ calculate the 75th term in the sequence.

Q10 Calculate the 34th term in the following sequences:

a) $1, \frac{1}{2}, \frac{1}{3}, \frac{1}{4}...$
b) 10, 20, 30, 40...
c) 0, 3, 8, 15, 24...
d) $1, x, x^2, x^3, x^4...$

Q11

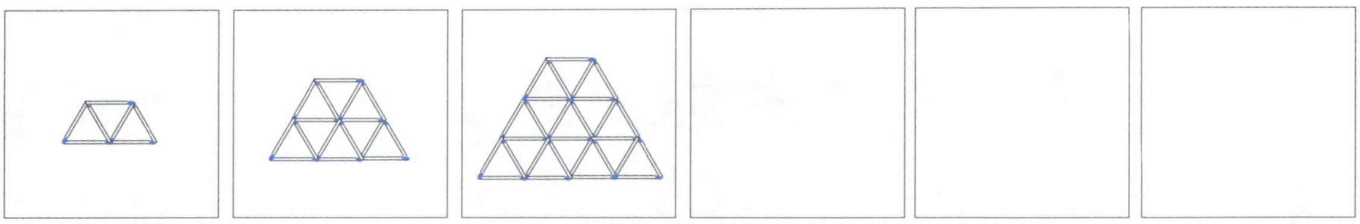

The pattern above is based on individual triangles.

a) Write down the number of triangles in each group.
b) Work out the number of triangles that would be in each of the next three groups.
c) Find a formula for the number of triangles in the nth term of the pattern.

Q12 A square tile pattern is formed with grey and white tiles. In the centre there is always a grey tile. The rest of the pattern is made up of grey and white tiles, with the four corner tiles of the square always being grey.
The first two patterns in the sequence are shown.

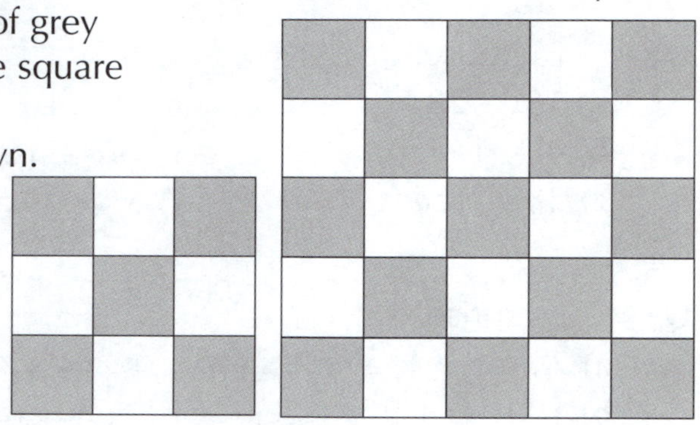

Work out the formula for:

a) the number of grey tiles in the 4th pattern.
b) the number of white tiles in the 4th pattern.
c) the total number of tiles in the nth pattern.

Q13 In the following sequences, write down the next 3 terms and the nth term:

a) 7, 10, 13, 16,...
b) 12, 17, 22, 27,...
c) 6, 16, 26, 36,...
d) 54, 61, 68, 75,...

Algebra

Q1 Multiply out the brackets and simplify your answers where possible:

a) $(x-3)(x+1)$
b) $(x-3)(x+5)$
c) $(x+10)(x+3)$
d) $(x-5)(x-2)$
e) $(x+2)(x-7)$
f) $(4-x)(7-x)$
g) $(2+3x)(3x-1)$
h) $(3x+2)(2x-4)$
i) $(x-3)(4x+1)$
j) $2(2x+y)(x-2y)$
k) $4(x+2y)(3x-2y)$
l) $(3x+2y)^2$

Q2 Find the product of $5x-2$ and $3x+2$.

Q3 Find the square of $2x-1$.

Q4 A rectangular pond has length $(3x-2)$ m and width $(5-x)$ m.
Write down a simplified expression for:

a) the pond's perimeter
b) the pond's area.

Q5 Find a simplified expression for the perimeter *and* the area of the following shapes.

a)

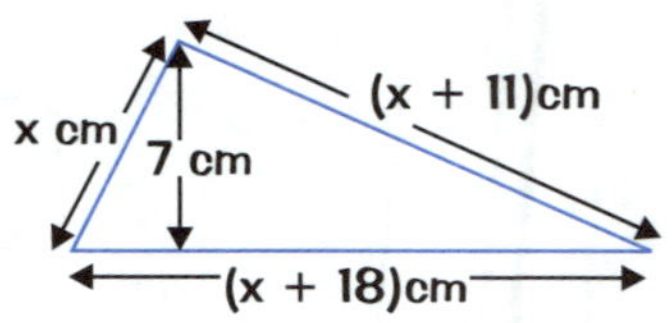

b)

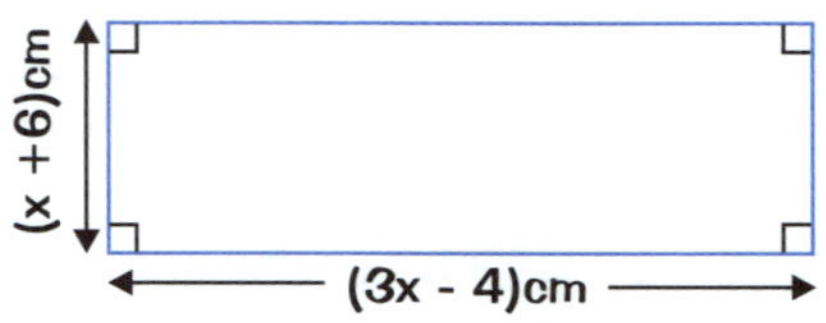

c)

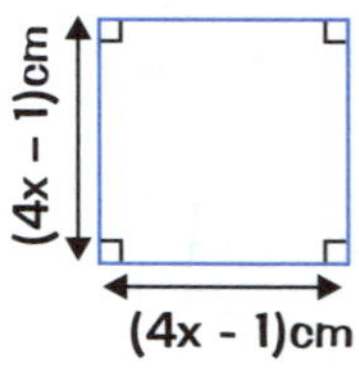

d)

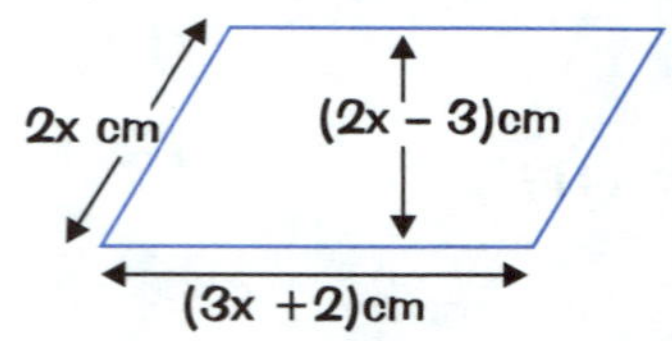

Q6 All the expressions below have a^2 as a common factor. Factorise each of them.

a) $a^2b + a^2c$
b) $5a^2 + 13a^2b$
c) $2a^2b + 3a^2c$
d) $a^3 + a^2y$
e) $2a^2x + 3a^2y + 4a^2z$
f) $a^2b^2 + a^3c^2$

Q7 Factorise each of the following completely.

a) $4x^2yz + 8xy^2z^3$ **b)** $64xy^4z + 12xyz$ **c)** $8xyz + 16x^2yz$ **d)** $20x^2y^2z^2 + 16xyz^2$

Q8 Factorise:

a) $16x - 28$
b) $4^2 - 14y$
c) $3q^2 - 12q$
d) $x^2 + 4x^2 + 2x$
e) $8b^3 + 16y^2 + 32t + 8$
f) $x^2y^2 - 3xy$
g) $p^3 + p^4$
h) $2ab^2 - 6a^2b^2 + 18abc$
i) $xy - y^2x + x^2y + x^2y^2$

Q9 Factorise:

a) $7a^2bc^2 + 14ab^2c + 21ab^2c^2 + 28a^2b^2c^2$
b) $100x^2yz + 90x^3yz + 80x^2y^2z + 70x^2yz + 60x^2yz^2$

Hmm, that last one looks a bit tricky — have a think about multiplying out brackets like at the top of the page.

Q10 Factorise:

a) $x^2 - 4$ **b)** $144 - y^4$ **c)** $1 - 9x^2y^2$ **d)** $49x^4y^4 - 1$

Algebraic Fractions

The trick for doing algebraic fractions is remembering how to do normal fractions — because they're just the same... in fact you can see at a glance if there's an x on the top and the bottom, so I reckon they're probably even easier.

Q1 Simplify the following by cancelling down where possible:

a) $\frac{27x^4y^2z}{9x^3yz^2}$ **b)** $\frac{48a^2b^2}{(2a)^2c}$ **c)** $\frac{48xyz}{9x^2y^3z^4}$ **d)** $\frac{4p^3q^3}{(2pr)^3}$

Q2 Multiply out the following, leaving your answer as simplified as possible:

a) $\frac{x^2}{y}\times\frac{2}{x^3}$

b) $\frac{3a^4}{2}\times\frac{b}{a^2}$

c) $\frac{2x}{y^2}\times\frac{y^3}{4x^3}$

d) $\frac{3pq}{2}\times\frac{4r^2}{9p}$

e) $\frac{10z^3}{xy}\times\frac{4x^3}{5z}$

f) $\frac{30a^2b^2c^2}{7}\times\frac{21c^2}{ab^3}$

g) $\frac{4}{x}\times\frac{x^3}{2}\times\frac{x}{10}$

h) $\frac{2a^2}{3}\times\frac{9b}{a}\times\frac{2a^2b}{5}$

i) $\frac{5a^2b}{b}\times\frac{3a^2c^3}{10bd}$

j) $\frac{p^2}{pq^2}\times\frac{q^2}{p}$

k) $\frac{90r^2}{14t}\times\frac{7t^3}{30r}$

l) $\frac{400d^4}{51e^5}\times\frac{102d^2e^4}{800e^2f}$

Q3 Divide the following, leaving your answer as simplified as possible:

a) $\frac{4x^3}{y}\div\frac{2x}{y^2}$

b) $\frac{ab}{c}\div\frac{b}{c}$

c) $\frac{30x^3}{y^2}\div\frac{10x}{y}$

d) $\frac{pq}{r}\div\frac{2}{r}$

e) $\frac{e^2f^2}{5}\div\frac{ef}{10}$

f) $\frac{5x^3}{y}\div\frac{1}{y}$

g) $\frac{16xyz}{3}\div\frac{4x^2}{9}$

h) $\frac{20a^2}{b^3}\div\frac{5}{b^2}$

i) $\frac{25a^3}{b^3}\div\frac{5}{b^2}$

j) $\frac{4x}{y^4z^4}\div\frac{2}{y^2z^3}$

k) $\frac{3m}{2n^2}\div\frac{m}{4n}$

l) $\frac{70f^3}{g}\div\frac{10f^4}{g^2}$

Q4 Solve the following equations for x:

a) $\frac{20x^4y^2z^3}{7xy^5}\times\frac{14y^3}{40x^2z^3}=5$ **b)** $\frac{48x^5y^2}{12z^3}\div\frac{16x^2y^2}{z^3}=2$

Algebraic Fractions

OK, I guess it gets a bit tricky here — you've got to cross-multiply to get a common denominator before you can get anywhere with adding or subtracting.

Q5 Add the following, simplifying your answers:

a) $\frac{3}{2x}+\frac{y}{2x}$

b) $\frac{1}{x}+\frac{y}{x}$

c) $\frac{4xy}{3z}+\frac{2xy}{3z}$

d) $\frac{4x+2}{3}+\frac{2x-1}{3}$

e) $\frac{5x+2}{x}+\frac{2x+4}{x}$

f) $\frac{6x}{3}+\frac{2x+y}{6}$

g) $\frac{x}{8}+\frac{2+y}{24}$

h) $\frac{x}{10}+\frac{y-1}{5}$

i) $\frac{2x}{3}+\frac{2x}{4}$

j) $\frac{x}{6}+\frac{5x}{7}$

k) $\frac{x}{3}+\frac{x}{y}$

l) $\frac{zx}{4}+\frac{x+z}{y}$

Q6 Subtract the following, leaving your answers as simplified as possible:

a) $\frac{4x}{3}-\frac{5y}{3}$

b) $\frac{4x+3}{y}-\frac{4}{y}$

c) $\frac{8x+3y}{2x}-\frac{4x+2}{2x}$

d) $\frac{9-5x}{3x}-\frac{3+x}{3x}$

e) $\frac{10+x^2}{4x}-\frac{x^2+11}{4x}$

f) $\frac{2x}{3}-\frac{y}{6}$

g) $\frac{z}{5}-\frac{2z}{15}$

h) $\frac{4m}{n}-\frac{m}{3}$

i) $\frac{2b}{a}-\frac{b}{7}$

j) $\frac{p+q}{2}-\frac{3p}{5}$

k) $\frac{p-2q}{4}-\frac{2p+q}{2}$

l) $\frac{3x}{y}-\frac{4-x}{3}$

Q7 Simplify the following:

a) $\left(\frac{a}{b}\div\frac{c}{d}\right)\times\frac{ac}{bd}$

b) $\frac{x^2+xy}{x}\times\frac{z}{xz+yz}$

c) $\frac{p+q}{r}\times\frac{3}{2(p+q)}$

d) $\frac{m^2n}{p}+\frac{mn}{p^2}$

e) $\frac{1}{x+y}+\frac{1}{x-y}$

f) $\frac{2}{x}-\frac{3}{2x}+\frac{4}{3x}$

g) $\frac{a+b}{a-b}+\frac{a-b}{a+b}$

h) $\frac{1}{4pq}\div\frac{1}{3pq}$

i) $\frac{x}{8}-\frac{x+y}{4}+\frac{x-y}{2}$

Speed, Distance and Time

I reckon this is pretty easy — it's just a case of taking your time, putting the right numbers into the speed formula triangle and getting the answer out. And don't forget to check your answer's in the right units.

Q1 **a)** A car travels 32 km in 40 mins. What is its average speed?
b) A train travels at an average speed of 96 km/h for 35 mins. How far has it travelled?
c) A cyclist travels 12 km at 16 km/h. How long does it take?

Q2 A car travels 8 km at an average speed of 30 km/h. Then it joins the motorway and travels 200 km at 104 km/h.
What is the average speed for the whole journey?

Q3 A main road through a town has a speed limit of 30 mph. A driver covers $2\frac{1}{4}$ miles through the centre in 4 mins. Did she break the speed limit?

Q4 A train leaves station A at 0915 and arrives at station B at 1005. If it travels at an average speed of 72 mph, how far apart are the stations?

Q5 This table shows the car mileage at various times on a journey.

Time	1410	1530	1655	1845	2040
Mileage	10537	10589	10655	10695	10780

a) What was the average speed between 1410 and 1530?
b) Between which times do you think a stop was made for refuelling and refreshments? Give a reason.
c) What was the average speed for the last section of the journey?
d) If the car does approximately 12 miles per litre of fuel, estimate how many litres were used on the journey.
e) What was the average speed for the whole journey?

Q6 A cyclist leaves home at 1430 and cycles at an average speed of 14 km/h to visit a friend. After one hour he stops for 20 mins then continues at an average speed of 11 km/h and arrives at his friend's house at 1700.
a) How far does he travel before the rest?
b) How far is it to his friend's house?
c) What was his average speed for the whole journey?

Speed, Distance and Time

Q7 The distance between two railway stations is 145 km.

a) How long does a train travelling at 65 km/h on average take to travel this distance?

b) Another train travels at an average speed of 80 km/h (when it's moving) but has a 10 min stop during the journey. How long does this second train take?

c) If both arrive at 1600, what time did each leave?

Q8 Two athletes run a road race. The first athlete ran at an average speed of 16 km/h, the second at 4 m/s. Which was the fastest? How long would each take to run 10 km?

Q9 A plane leaves Amsterdam at 0715 and flies at an average speed of 650 km/h to Paris, arriving at 0800. It takes off again at 0840 and flies at the same average speed to Nice, arriving at 1005.

a) How far is it from Amsterdam to Paris?

b) How far is it from Paris to Nice?

c) What was the average speed for the whole journey?

Remember, for the average speed, you use the total time and the total distance.

Q10 A runner covered the first 100 m of a 200 m race in 12.3 seconds.

a) What was his average speed for the first 100 m?

b) The second 100 m took 15.1 seconds. What was the average speed for 200 m?

Q11 A military plane can achieve a speed of 1100 km/h. At this speed it passes over town A at 1205 and town B at 1217.

a) How far apart are towns A and B?

b) The plane then flies over village C, which is 93 km from B. How long does it take from B to C?

Q12 Two cars set off on 180 mile journeys. One travels mostly on A roads and manages an average speed of 42 mph. The other car travels mostly on the motorway and achieves an average speed while moving of 64 mph. If they both take the same time over the journey, for how long does the second car stop?

Q13 A stone is dropped from a cliff top. After 1 second it has fallen 4.8 m, after 2 seconds a total of 19.2 m and after 3 seconds 43.2 m. Calculate its average speed in:

a) the first second

b) the second second

c) for all 3 seconds

d) Change all the m/s speeds to km/h.

Q14 In 1990 three motor racers had average speeds of 236.6, 233.8 and 227.3 km/h. If 1 km = 0.62 miles, how long would each driver take to complete a 5-mile lap?

Solving Equations

Q1 When 1 is added to a number and the answer then trebled, it gives the same result as doubling the number and then adding 4. Find the number.

Q2 Solve the following:

a) $2x^2 = 18$ **b)** $2x^2 = 72$ **c)** $3x^2 = 27$ **d)** $4x^2 = 36$ **e)** $5x^2 = 5$

Q3 Solve the following:

a) $3x + 1 = 2x + 6$
b) $4x + 3 = 3x + 7$
c) $5x - 1 = 3x + 19$
d) $\frac{1}{2}x + 2 = x - 1$
e) $x + 15 = 4x$
f) $3x^2 + 3 = 2x^2 + 12$

Q4 Mary is y years old. Her father is 4 times older than Mary. Her mother is 7 years younger than her father. If their three ages add up to 101 years, find the value of y. Find the ages of Mary's parents.

Q5 Solve:

a) $2(x - 3) - (x - 2) = 5$
b) $5(x + 2) - 3(x - 5) = 29$
c) $2(x + 2) + 3(x + 4) = 31$
d) $10(x + 3) - 4(x - 2) = 7(x + 5)$
e) $5(4x + 3) = 4(7x - 5) + 3(9 - 2x)$
f) $3(7 + 2x) + 2(1 - x) = 19$
g) $\frac{x}{3} + 7 = 12$
h) $\frac{x}{10} + 18 = 29$
i) $17 - \frac{x^2}{3} = 5$
j) $41 - \frac{x}{11} = 35$
k) $\frac{x}{100} - 3 = 4$
l) $\frac{120}{x} = 16$

Q6 Joan, Kate and Linda win £2,400 on the National Lottery between them. Joan gets a share of £x, whilst Kate gets twice as much as Joan. Linda's share is £232 less than Joan's amount.

a) Write down an expression for the amounts Joan, Kate and Linda win.
b) Write down an equation in terms of x, and solve it.
c) Write down the amounts Kate and Linda receive.

Q7 Two men are decorating a room. One has painted 20 m^2 and the other only 6 m^2. They continue painting and both manage to paint another x m^2 each. If the first man has painted exactly three times the area painted by the second man, find the value of x.

Q8 Solve the following:

a) $\frac{y}{2} + 2 = 13$
b) $\frac{3x}{4} - 2 = 4$
c) $\frac{2z}{5} - 3 = -5$
d) $\frac{1}{5}(x - 4) = 3$
e) $\frac{2}{3}(x + 1) = 16$
f) $\frac{3}{5}(4x - 3) = 15$
g) $\frac{8}{x^2} = \frac{32}{36}$
h) $\frac{12}{5x^2} = \frac{3}{20}$
i) $\frac{14}{3x^2} = \frac{2}{21}$

Q9 A triangle has lengths as shown below. Find the length of each side, if the length of AC exceeds that of AB by $\frac{1}{2}$ cm.

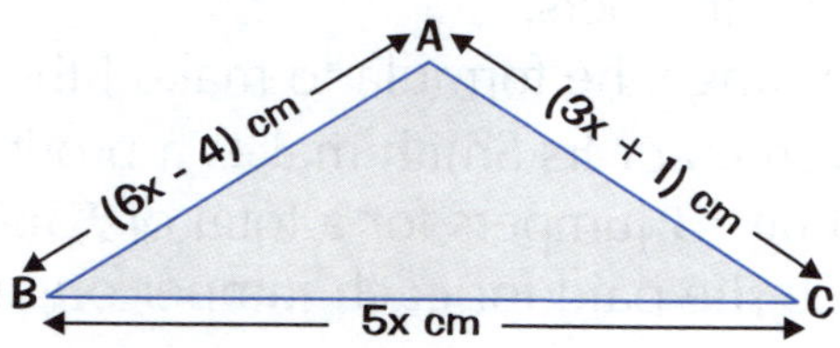

Rearranging Formulas

Rearranging is getting the letter you want out of the formula and making it the subject. And it's exactly the same method as for solving equations, which can't be bad.

Q1 Rearrange the following formulas to make the letter in brackets the new subject.

a) $y = x^2 - 2$ (x)

b) $y = \sqrt{(x+3)}$ (x)

c) $r = \left(\frac{s}{2}\right)^2$ (s)

d) $f = \frac{10+g}{3}$ (g)

e) $w = \frac{5-z}{2}$ (z)

f) $v = \frac{1}{3}x^2h$ (x)

g) $v^2 = u^2 + 2as$ (a)

h) $v^2 = u^2 + 2as$ (u)

i) $t = 2\pi\sqrt{\frac{1}{g}}$ (g)

Q2 The cost of hiring a car is £28 per day plus 25p per mile.

a) Find the cost of hiring the car and travelling:

i) 40 miles.

ii) 80 miles.

b) Write down a formula to give the cost of hiring a car (£) for one day, and travelling n miles.

c) Rearrange the formula to make n the subject.

d) How many miles can you travel, during one day, if you have a budget of:

i) £34, **ii)** £50, **iii)** £56.50.

Q3 Rearrange the following formulas, by collecting terms in x and looking for common factors, to make x the new subject:

a) $xy = z - 2x$

b) $ax = 3x + b$

c) $4x - y = xz$

d) $xy = 3z - 5x + y$

e) $xy = xz - 2$

f) $2(x - y) = z(x + 3)$

g) $xyz = x - y - wz$

h) $3y(x + z) = y(2z - x)$

These are getting quite tricky — you've got to <u>collect like terms</u>, before you can make anything else the subject.

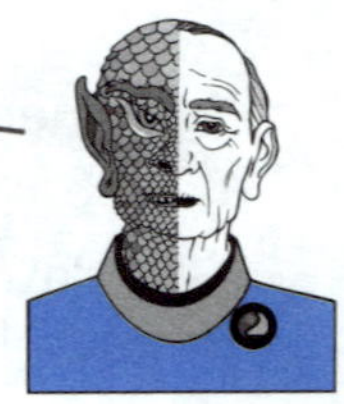

Q4 Rearrange the following formulas to make y the new subject.

a) $y(x - 1) = x$

b) $x(y + 2) = y - 3$

c) $x = \frac{y^2+1}{2y^2-1}$

d) $x = \frac{2y^2+1}{3y^2-1}$

Q5 Mrs Smith buys x jumpers for £J each and sells them in her shop for a total price of £T.

a) Write down an expression for the amount of money she paid for all the jumpers.

b) Using your answer to **a)**, write down a formula for the profit £P Mrs Smith makes selling all the jumpers.

c) Rearrange the formula to make J the subject.

d) Given that Mrs Smith makes a profit of £156 by selling 13 jumpers for a total of £364, find the price she paid for each jumper originally.

Inequalities

Yet another one of those bits of Maths that looks worse than it is — these are just like equations, really, except for the symbols.

Q1 Write down the inequality represented by each diagram below.

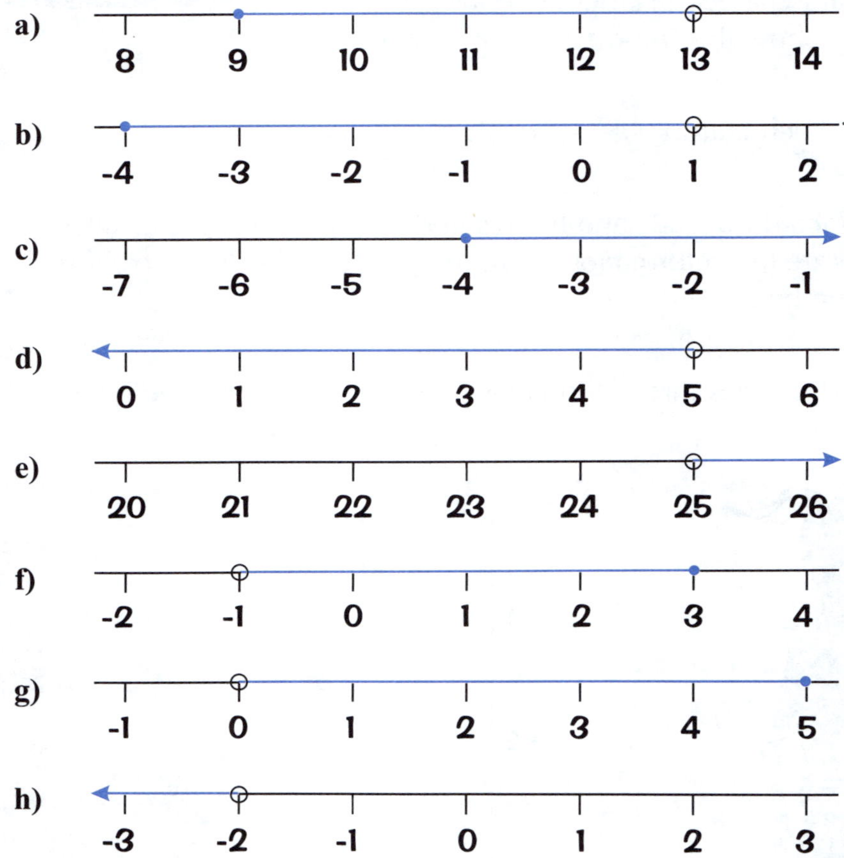

A solid circle means the value at that point <u>is</u> included. A hollow circle means the value isn't included.

Q2 By drawing an appropriate part of the number line for each question, represent each of the following inequalities:

a) $x > 5$
b) $x \leqslant 2$
c) $2 > x > -5$
d) $3 > x \geqslant -2$
e) $3 \geqslant x > -2$
f) $7 \geqslant x > 6$
g) $-3 \leqslant x \leqslant -2$
h) $0 \geqslant x > -3$

Q3 Draw and label a number line from –5 to 5 for each of the following questions. Represent the inequalities on your number lines.

a) $x^2 \leqslant 4$
b) $x^2 < 1$
c) $x^2 \leqslant 9$
d) $25 \geqslant x^2$
e) $16 \geqslant x^2$
f) $x^2 \leqslant 1$
g) $9 > x^2$
h) $x^2 \leqslant 0$

Q4 Solve the following:

a) $3x + 2 > 11$
b) $5x + 4 < 24$
c) $5x + 7 \leqslant 32$
d) $3x + 12 \leqslant 30$
e) $2x - 7 \geqslant 8$
f) $17 + 4x < 33$
g) $2(x + 3) < 20$
h) $2(5x - 4) < 32$
i) $5(x + 2) \geqslant 25$
j) $4(x - 1) > 40$
k) $10 - 2x > 4x - 8$
l) $7 - 2x \leqslant 4x + 10$
m) $8 - 3x \geqslant 14$
n) $16 - x < 11$
o) $16 - x > 1$
p) $12 - 3x \leqslant 18$

Inequalities

Q5 There are 1,130 pupils in a school. No class must have more than 32 pupils. How many classrooms are needed? Show this information as an inequality.

Q6 A person is prepared to spend £300 taking friends out to celebrate. If the restaurant charges £12 per head, how many guests could be invited? Show this information as an inequality.

Q7 Find the largest integer x such that $2x + 5 \geqslant 5x - 2$.

Q8 When a number is subtracted from 11, and the result divided by two, the answer is always less than five. Write this information as an inequality and solve it to show the possible values of the number.

Q9 The shaded region below satisfies three inequalities. Write down the three inequalities.

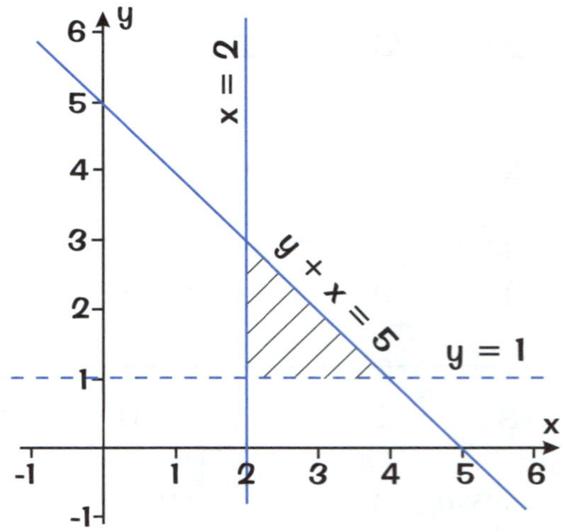

Q10 Draw a set of axes with the x-axis from –2 to 6 and the y-axis from –1 to 7. Show on a graph the region enclosed by the following three inequalities:

$$y < 6 \quad , \quad x + y \geqslant 5 \quad \text{and} \quad x \leqslant 5$$

Q11 Draw a set of axes with the x-axis from 0 to 8 and the y-axis from 0 to 10. Show on a graph the region enclosed by the following three inequalities:

$$x > 1 \quad , \quad x + y \leqslant 7 \quad \text{and} \quad y \geqslant 2$$

Q12 Draw a set of axes with the x-axis from –4 to 5 and the y-axis from –3 to 6. Show on a graph the region enclosed by the following:

$$y \leqslant 2x + 4 \quad , \quad y < 5 - x \quad \text{and} \quad y \geqslant \frac{x}{3} - 1$$

Factorising Quadratics

It's factorising Jim, but not as we know it... Better watch out with these, I reckon.

Q1 Factorise the following:

a) $x^2 + 11x + 24$
b) $x^2 + 15x + 36$
c) $x^2 + 13x + 36$
d) $x^2 + 16x + 48$
e) $x^2 + 14x + 48$
f) $x^2 + 26x + 48$
g) $x^2 + 49x + 48$
h) $x^2 + 19x + 48$
i) $x^2 + 3x$
j) $2x - x^2$
k) $x^2 + 4x$
l) $x^2 - 20x$
m) $x^2 + 10x$
n) $9x + x^2$
o) $x^2 + x - 6$
p) $x^2 - x - 12$
q) $x^2 - 5x + 6$
r) $x^2 - 6x + 8$
s) $x^2 - 11x + 28$
t) $x^2 - 2x - 35$
u) $x^2 - 3x - 40$
v) $x^2 + 10x - 24$
w) $x^2 - 15x + 44$
x) $x^2 - 11x - 26$.

Your best bet with these is the old guessing game. Come up with a pair of numbers, then try adding and multiplying them.

Remember, they've got to multiply together to make the number at the end and add together to make the x term in the middle.

Q2 Solve the following quadratic equations:

a) $(x + 2)(x + 8) = 0$
b) $(3 - x)(4 - x) = 0$
c) $(x + 4)(x + 18) = 0$
d) $(x - 2)(x - 2) = 0$
e) $(x + 3)^2 = 0$
f) $(x - 9)^2 = 0$
g) $(x + 4)^2 = 0$
h) $(x - 25)^2 = 0$
i) $x(x + 4) = 0$
j) $x(x - 7) = 0$
k) $x(x + 30) = 0$
l) $x(x + 2) = 0$.

Q3 Factorise the quadratics first, and then solve the equations:

a) $x^2 + 3x - 10 = 0$
b) $x^2 - 5x + 6 = 0$
c) $x^2 - 2x + 1 = 0$
d) $x^2 - 4x + 3 = 0$
e) $x^2 - x - 20 = 0$
f) $x^2 - 4x - 5 = 0$
g) $x^2 + 6x - 7 = 0$
h) $x^2 + 14x + 49 = 0$
i) $x^2 - 2x - 15 = 0$.

Q4 A rug has length x m. The width is exactly 1 m less than the length.

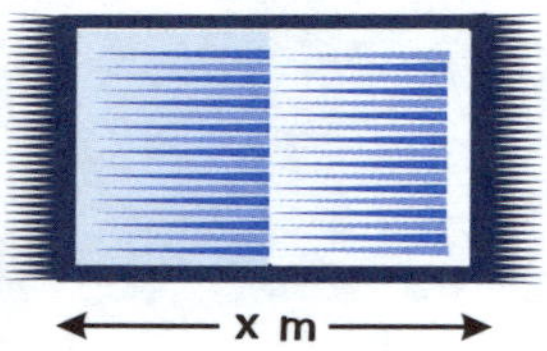

a) Write down an expression for the area of the rug.
b) If the area of the rug is 6 m² find the value of x.

Q5 Use "the difference of two squares" to solve these quadratics:

a) $x^2 - 9 = 0$
b) $x^2 - 16 = 0$
c) $4x^2 - 36 = 0$
d) $9x^2 - 49 = 0$.

Q6 **a)** When x is added to its square, the total is 12. Find the values of x.
b) When y is subtracted from its square, the total is 12. Find the values of y.

Q7 The area of a rectangular swimming pool is 28 m². The width is x m. The difference between the length and width is 3 m. Find the value of x.

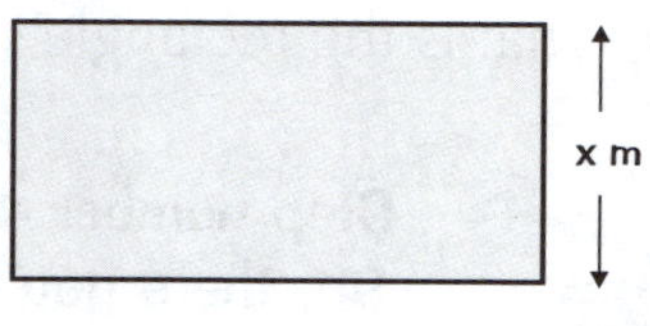

Q8 Solve: **a)** $x + 21 = \frac{9(x-3)}{x}$ **b)** $x^2 - \frac{1}{4} = 0$

The Quadratic Formula

Q1 Find the two values, to 2 d.p., given by each of the following expressions:

a) $\frac{2\pm\sqrt{3}}{2}$

b) $\frac{4\pm\sqrt{10}}{3}$

c) $\frac{-2\pm\sqrt{27}}{2}$

d) $\frac{-3\pm\sqrt{42}}{3}$

e) $\frac{-10\pm\sqrt{160}}{5}$

f) $\frac{-27\pm\sqrt{10}}{2}$

g) $\frac{-8\pm\sqrt{9.5}}{2.4}$

h) $\frac{10\pm\sqrt{88.4}}{23.2}$

Step number 1 on the stairway to spiritual fulfilment... learn the Quadratic Formula.

Q2 The following quadratics can be solved by factorisation, but practise using the formula to solve them:

a) $x^2 + 8x + 12 = 0$
b) $6x^2 - x - 2 = 0$
c) $x^2 - x - 6 = 0$
d) $x^2 - 3x + 2 = 0$
e) $4x^2 - 15x + 9 = 0$
f) $x^2 - 3x = 0$
g) $36x^2 - 48x + 16 = 0$
h) $x^2 + x - 20 = 0$
i) $4x^2 + 8x - 12 = 0$
j) $3x^2 - 11x - 20 = 0$
k) $x + 3 = 2x^2$
l) $5 - 3x - 2x^2 = 0$
m) $1 - 5x + 6x^2 = 0$
n) $3(x^2 + 2x) = 9$

Step number 2... Beware The Minus Signs

Step number 3... divide <u>the whole</u> of the top line by 2*a*, <u>not just $\frac{1}{2}$ of it</u> — and remember it's <u>2*a*</u>, not just <u>*a*</u>.

Q3 Solve the following quadratics using the formula. Give your answers to no more than two decimal places.

a) $x^2 + 3x - 1 = 0$
b) $x^2 - 2x - 6 = 0$
c) $x^2 + x - 1 = 0$
d) $x^2 + 6x + 3 = 0$
e) $x^2 + 5x + 2 = 0$
f) $x^2 + 4x + 2 = 0$
g) $x^2 - 6x - 8 = 0$
h) $x^2 - 14x + 11 = 0$
i) $x^2 + 3x - 5 = 0$
j) $7x^2 - 15x + 6 = 0$

Q4 The area of a rectangle with length $(x + 4.6)$ cm and width $(x - 2.1)$ cm is 134.63 cm^2.

a) Form a quadratic equation and solve it to find x to two decimal places.

b) What is the rectangle's perimeter to one decimal place?

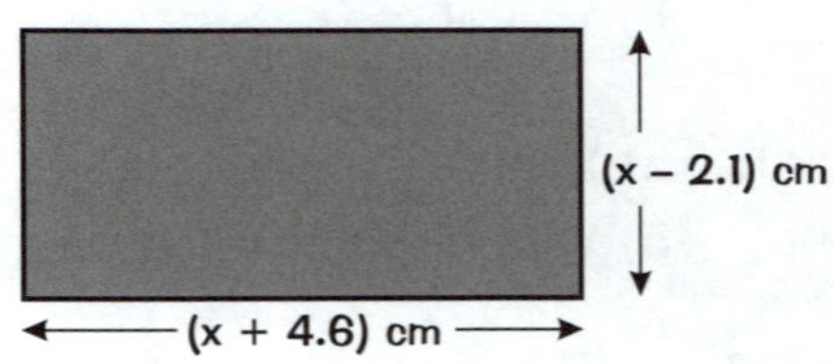

Step number 4... check your answers by putting them <u>back in the equation</u>. So, there you have it — spiritual fulfilment... or as close as you'll get to it within a 5 mile radius of a quadratic equation.

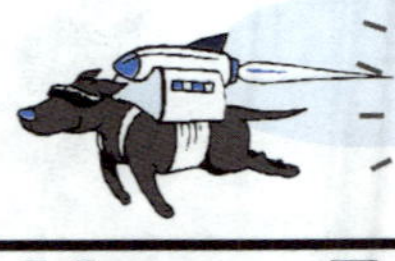

Completing the Square

All you're doing is writing it in the form "(x + 4)² + 2" instead of "x² + 8x + 18" — don't let the name put you off.

Q1 Complete the square for the following expressions:

a) $x^2 - 4x - 5$
b) $x^2 - 2x + 1$
c) $x^2 + x + 1$
d) $x^2 - 6x + 9$
e) $x^2 - 6x + 7$
f) $x^2 - 4x$
g) $x^2 + 3x - 4$
h) $x^2 - x - 3$
i) $x^2 - 10x + 25$
j) $x^2 - 10x$
k) $x^2 + 8x + 17$
l) $x^2 - 12x + 35$

Q2 Solve the following quadratic equations by completing the square. Write down your answers to no more than 2 d.p.

a) $x^2 + 3x - 1 = 0$
b) $x^2 - x - 3 = 0$
c) $x^2 + 4x - 3 = 0$
d) $x^2 + x - 1 = 0$
e) $x^2 - 3x - 5 = 0$
f) $2x^2 - 6x + 1 = 0$
g) $3x^2 - 3x - 2 = 0$
h) $3x^2 - 6x - 1 = 0$

It's quite a cunning method, really... but I admit it takes a bit of getting used to — make sure you've learnt all the steps, then it's just practice, practice...

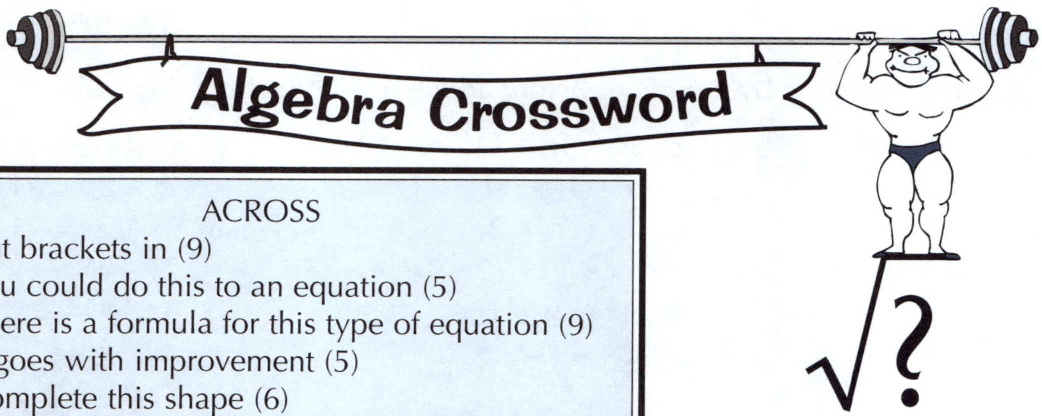

ACROSS

1 Put brackets in (9)
5 You could do this to an equation (5)
6 There is a formula for this type of equation (9)
9 It goes with improvement (5)
10 Complete this shape (6)

DOWN

1 You should rearrange these (8)
2 $x \leqslant -6$ is an example of an ________ (10)
3 $2x + 4 = 6$ is one (8)
4 Some things grow, others ________ (5)
7 It's a type of proportion (7)
8 These are found a lot in algebra (and post boxes) (7)

Simultaneous Equations

To solve simultaneous equations from scratch, you've got to get rid of either x or y first — to leave you with an equation with just one unknown in it.

Q1 Eliminate either the x term or the y term by adding or subtracting the pairs of equations, and hence solve the equations:

a) $4x - y = 13$
$2x - y = 5$

b) $8x + 3y = 8$
$5x - 3y = 5$

c) $x + 3y = 10$
$2x - 3y = 2$

d) $8x + 6y = 2$
$2(x - 3y) = 3$

e) $x - 12y = 16$
$5x + 12y = 8$

f) $2(5x - y + 4) = 0$
$10x + y = 19$

g) $11x + 3y = 5$
$7x - 3y = 13$

h) $2x + 7y = 11$
$2x + 3y = 7$

i) $x + 6y = 5$
$3(x + 2y - 1) = 0$

Q2 Rearrange the equations before solving for x and y:

a) $3y - 4 = 10$
$4(x - \frac{y}{2} + 2) = 0$

b) $3x + y = 13$
$2y - 3x = 8$

c) $3y + 4x = 10$
$4x - 2y + 8 = 0$

d) $y + 1 = 3x$
$y - x = 3$

e) $y + x = 2$
$y - \frac{1}{2}x + 1 = 0$

f) $y - 3 = 2x$
$y = x - 1$

g) $4y - 3x = 22$
$3x - 2y = -14$

h) $y + 2x = 5$
$y = x - 4$

i) $2y + x = 2$
$y + x + 1 = 0$

j) $3y + 2x = 19$
$2x + y = 1$

k) $9x - y = 12$
$4y - 9x = 6$

l) $6x + 2y = 5$
$3y - 6x = 15$

Q3 Multiply one equation by a number before adding or subtracting, then solve the equations:

a) $3x + 2y = 12$
$2x + y = 7$

b) $5x - y = 17$
$2x + 3y = 0$

c) $x + 3y = 11$
$2x + 5y = 19$

d) $5x + 3y = 24$
$x + 5y = -4$

e) $3x + 2y = 3$
$2x + y = 23$

f) $4x + 2y = 8$
$x + 3y = 2$

g) $x + 14y = -2$
$2x + 3y = 21$

h) $3x + 2y = 21$
$2x - y = 7$

i) $4x - y = -2$
$3x - 2y = 1$

Q4 Multiply both equations by a number before adding or subtracting, to solve these:

a) $7y - 3x = 2$
$5y - 2x = 2$

b) $5x - 8y = 12$
$4x - 7y = 9$

c) $4x - 2y = -6$
$5x + 3y = 20$

d) $7x + 5y = 66$
$3x - 4y = 16$

e) $10x + 4y = 2$
$8x + 3y = 1$

f) $3x + 4y = 19$
$4x - 3y = -8$

Q5 Use the linear equation (the one with no x^2s in it) to find an expression for y. Then substitute it into the quadratic equation (the one with x^2s in it), to solve these equations:

a) $y = x^2 + 2$
$y = x + 14$

b) $y = x^2 - 8$
$y = 3x + 10$

c) $y = 2x^2$
$y = x + 3$

d) $x + 5y = 30$
$x^2 + \frac{4}{5}x = y$

e) $y = 1 - 13x$
$y = 4x^2 + 4$

f) $y = 3(x^2 + 3)$
$14x + y = 1$

For question 5, you'll get two possible values for x. Which means you'll also have two possible values for y...

Simultaneous Equations

Each time you do a step, write it down — "Multiply A by 2" — that sort of thing. I know it sounds a waste of time, but if you mess it up, it'll be easier to check what went wrong.

Q6 Solve the following simultaneous equations:

a) $4x + 6y = 16$
$x + 2y = 5$

b) $3x + 8y = 24$
$x + y = 3$

c) $3y - 8x = 24$
$3y + 2x = 9$

Careful with parts d) to f) — some of them are quadratics...

d) $y = x^2 - 2$
$y = 3x + 8$

e) $y = 3x^2 - 10$
$13x - y = 14$

f) $y + 2 = 2x^2$
$y + 3x = 0$

g) $3y - 10x - 17 = 0$
$\frac{1}{3}y + 3x - 6 = 0$

h) $\frac{x}{2} - 2y = 5$
$12y + x - 2 = 0$

i) $x + y = \frac{1}{2}(y - x)$
$x + y = 2$

Q7 Two numbers have a sum of 15 and a difference of 3. Write down a pair of simultaneous equations using x and y, and solve them.

Q8 Two numbers have a sum of 4 and a difference of 12. Write down a pair of simultaneous equations using x and y, and solve them.

Q9 A farmer has a choice of buying 6 sheep and 5 pigs for £430 or 4 sheep and 10 pigs for £500 at auction.

a) If sheep cost £x and pigs cost £y, write down his two choices as a pair of simultaneous equations.

b) Solve for x and y.

Q10 Six apples and four oranges cost £1.90, whereas eight apples and two oranges cost £1.80. Find the cost of an apple and the cost of an orange.

Q11 Find the value of x and y for each of the following rectangles, by first writing down a pair of simultaneous equations and then solving them.

a)
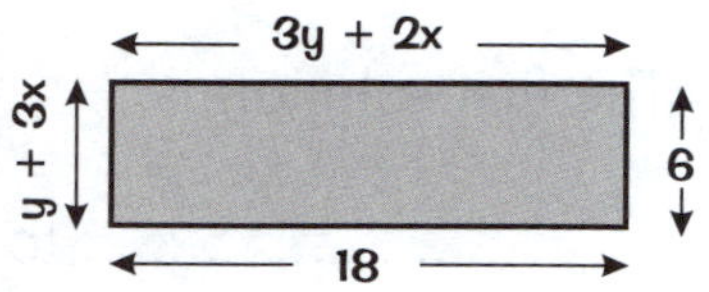

b)
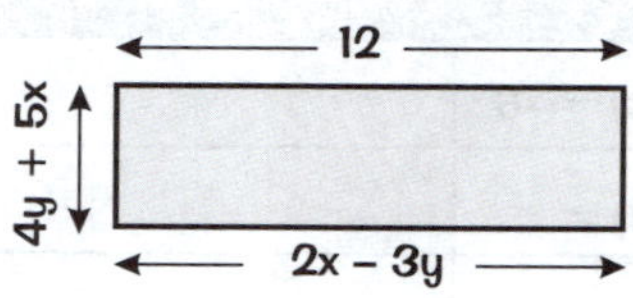

c)
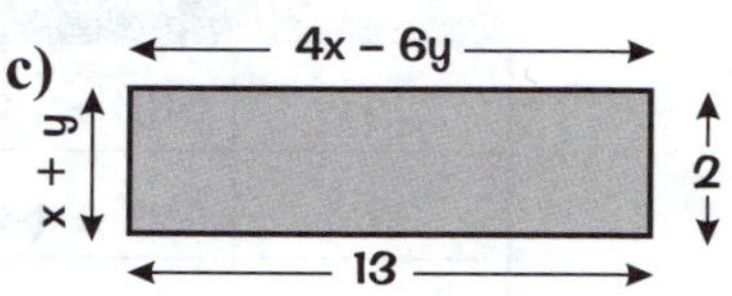

Q12 Two customers enter a shop to buy milk and cornflakes. Mrs Smith buys 5 pints of milk and 2 boxes of cornflakes and spends £3.44. Mr brown buys 4 pints of milk and 3 boxes of cornflakes and receives £6.03 change after paying with a £10 note. Write down a pair of simultaneous equations and solve them to find the price in pence of a pint of milk (m) and a box of cornflakes (c).

Q13 Three pens and seven pencils cost £1.31 whereas eight pencils and six pens cost £1.96. Find the cost of each.

Q14 Solve $\frac{3(x-y)}{5} = x - 3y = x - 6$.

Trial and Improvement

Q1 The cubic equation $x^3 + x = 24$ has a solution between 2 and 3. Copy the table below and use it to find this solution to 1 d.p.

Guess(x)	Value of $x^3 + x$	Too large or Too small
2	$2^3 + 2 =$	
3	$3^3 + 3 =$	

Q2 The cubic equation $x^3 - x^2 + x = 7$ has a solution between 2 and 3. Copy the table and use it to find this solution to 1 d.p.

Guess(x)	Value of $x^3 - x^2 + x$	Too large or Too small
2	$(2)^3 - (2)^2 + (2) =$	
3	$(3)^3 - (3)^2 + (3) =$	

Q3 The cubic equation $x^3 - x^2 = 0.7$ has a solution between 1 and 2. Copy the table on the right and use it to find this solution to 1 d.p.

Guess(x)	Value of $x^3 - x^2$	Too large or Too small
1	$(1)^3 - (1)^2 =$	
2	$(2)^3 - (2)^2 =$	

Q4 The cubic equation $x^3 + x^2 - 4x = 3$ has three solutions. The first solution lies between –3 and –2. The second lies between –1 and 0. The third solution lies between 1 and 2.

Guess(x)	Value of $x^3 + x^2 - 4x$	Too large or Too small
–3	$(-3)^3 + (-3)^2 - 4(-3) = -6$	
–2	$(-2)^3 + (-2)^2 - 4(-2) =$	
–1	$(-1)^3 + (-1)^2 - 4(-1) =$	
0	$(0)^3 + (0)^2 - 4(0) =$	
1	$(1)^3 + (1)^2 - 4(1) =$	
2	$(2)^3 + (2)^2 - 4(2) =$	

The first solution is

.... to 1 d.p.

The second solution is

.... to 1 d.p.

The third solution is

.... to 1 d.p.

They don't always give you the starting numbers — so if this happens, make sure you pick two opposite cases (one too big, one too small), or you've blown it.

Straight Lines

Keep learning these straight lines till they start coming out of your ears — you've got to know about the vertical/horizontal lines and the sloping ones through the origin.

Q1 Make a copy of this diagram:

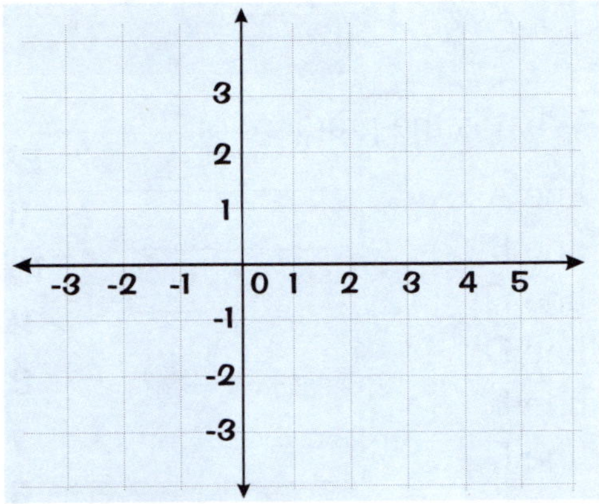

a) Label the x-axis.
b) Label the y-axis.
c) Draw the line $x = 3$.
d) Draw the line $y = 2$.
e) Draw and label the line $x + y = 0$.
f) Draw and label the line $x - y = 0$.

Q2 Make a copy of this diagram:

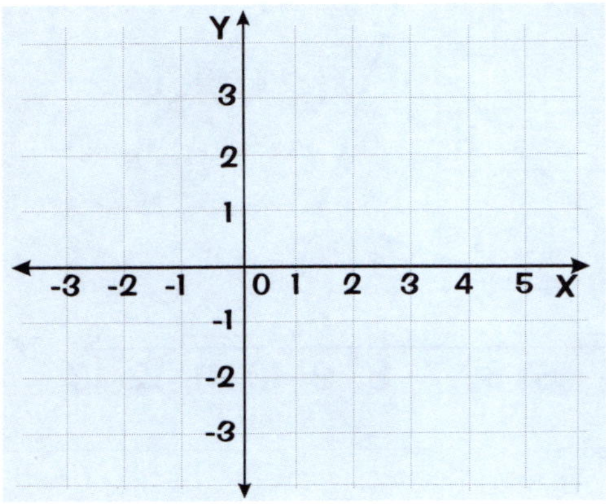

a) Label the line $x = 0$.
b) Label the line $y = 0$.
c) Draw and label the line $y = x$.
d) Draw and label the line $y = -x$.
e) Draw the line $x = -3$.
f) Draw the line $y = -2$.

Q3 Which letters represent the following lines:

a) $x = y$
b) $x = 5$
c) $y = -x$
d) $x = 0$
e) $y = -7$
f) $x + y = 0$
g) $y = 5$
h) $x - y = 0$
i) $y = 0$
j) $x = -7$?

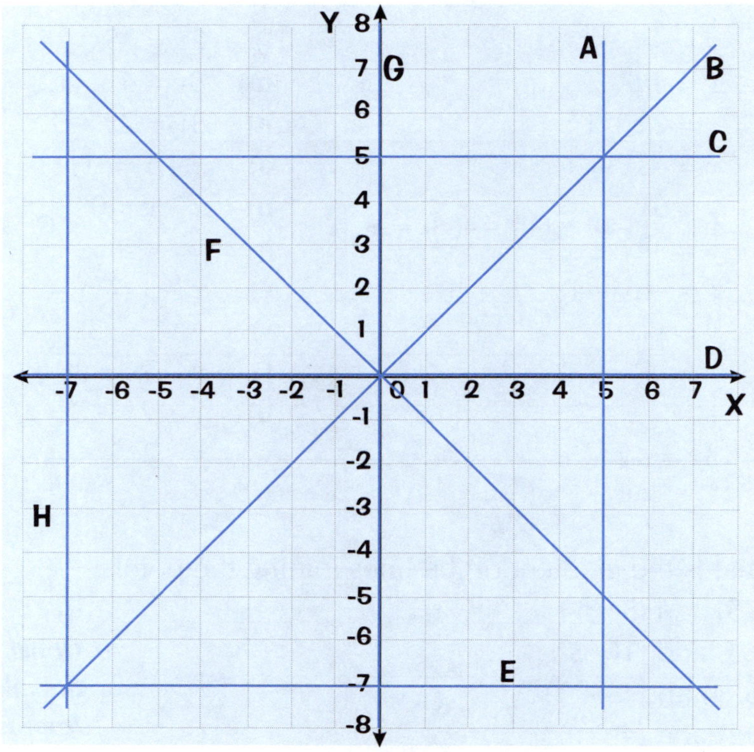

Don't get confused if you've got "$x + y = ...$ " — just rearrange the equation to "$y = -x + ...$" and as if by magic, you've got a line you recognise.

Straight-Line Graphs: $y = mx + c$

This page gives you plenty of practice finding the gradient and y-intercept of straight-line graphs. If you learn it now, it'll save you loads of time in the exam. Anything for an easy life...

Q1 What is the gradient of:

a) line A
b) line B
c) line C
d) line D
e) line E
f) line F
g) line G
h) line H
i) line I
j) line J?

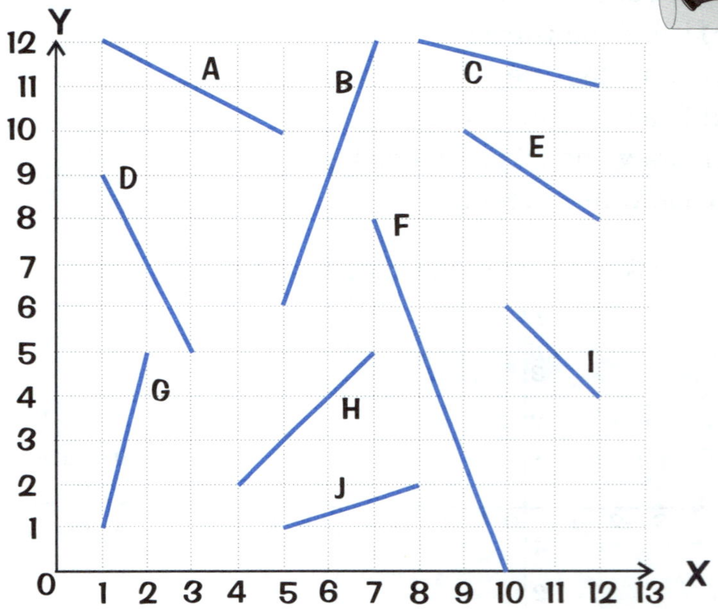

I know these are a bit more algebra-ish, but don't worry, they won't bite.

Q2 For each of the following lines, give the gradient and the coordinates of the point where the line cuts the y-axis:

a) $y = 4x + 3$
b) $y = 3x - 2$
c) $y = 2x + 1$
d) $y = -3x + 3$
e) $y = 5x$
f) $y = -2x + 3$
g) $y = -6x - 4$
h) $y = x$
i) $y = -\frac{1}{2}x + 3$
j) $y = \frac{1}{4}x + 2$
k) $3y = 4x + 6$
l) $2y = -5x - 4$
m) $8y = 4x - 12$
n) $3y = 7x + 5$
o) $x + y = 0$
p) $x - y = 0$
q) $y - x = 3$
r) $x - 3 = y$
s) $y - 7 = 3x$
t) $y - 5x = 3$
u) $y + 2x + 3 = 0$
v) $y - 2x - 4 = 0$

Q3 What is the gradient of the lines joining the points:

a) (3, 5) and (5, 9)
b) (6, 3) and (10, 5)
c) (–6, 4) and (–3, 1)
d) (8, 2) and (4, 10)
e) (8, 5) and (6, 4)
f) (–3, –1) and (1, –4)?

Uphill gradients are always positive, downhill always negative. Impressed? Hmmm....thought not. Can be a bit of an uphill battle, these.

Straight-Line Graphs: $y = mx + c$

Q4 Find the equations of the following lines:

a) A
b) B
c) C
d) D
e) E
f) F

Yeah, OK, this sounds a bit scary, but just work out the gradient (m) and look at the y-intercept (c) and pop them back into "y = mx + c"... easy lemons.

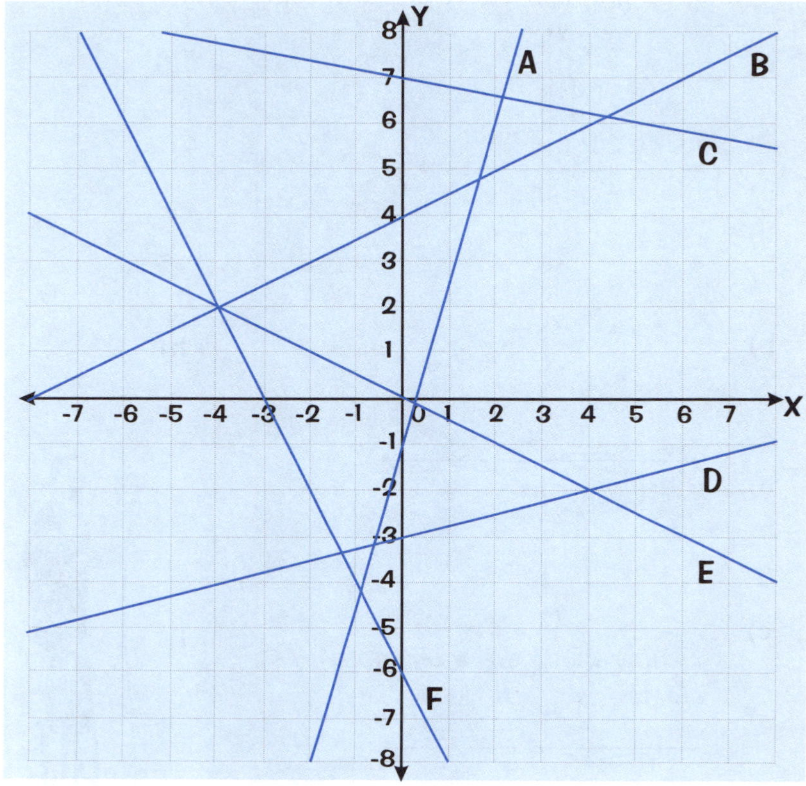

Q5 Find the equation of the straight line which passes through:

a) (3, 7) and has a gradient of 1
b) (2, 8) and has a gradient of 3
c) (–3, 3) and has a gradient of 2
d) (4, –4) and has a gradient of –1
e) (–1, 7) and has a gradient of –3
f) (4, –11) and has a gradient of –2.

Here's a bit more practice with those gradients. Thought you'd like that.

Q6 Write down the equation of the line which passes through the points:

a) (2, 2) and (5, 5)
b) (1, 3) and (4, 12)
c) (–2, –3) and (5, 11)
d) (1, 0) and (5, –12)
e) (–5, 6) and (–1, –2)
f) (4, 23) and (–2, –7).

Q7 What is the value of x or y if:

a) the point $(x, 13)$ is on the line $y = 3x + 1$
b) the point $(x, -2)$ is on the line $y = \frac{1}{2}x - 6$
c) the point $(4, y)$ is on the line $y = 2x - 1$
d) the point $(-3, y)$ is on the line $y = -3x$?

Q8 Which of the following points lie on the line $y = 3x - 1$?
(7, 20), (6, 15), (5, 14)

Graphs to Recognise

Q1 Identify the type of graph shown below. Choose from straight-line, quadratic (x^2 bucket-shaped graphs), cubic (x^3) and reciprocal ($1/x$):

a)

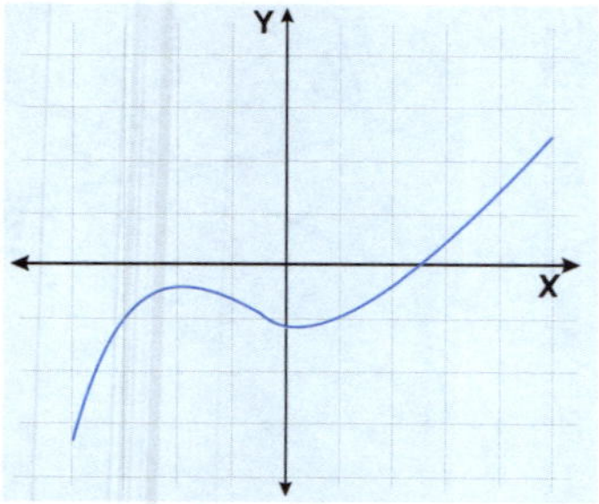

b)

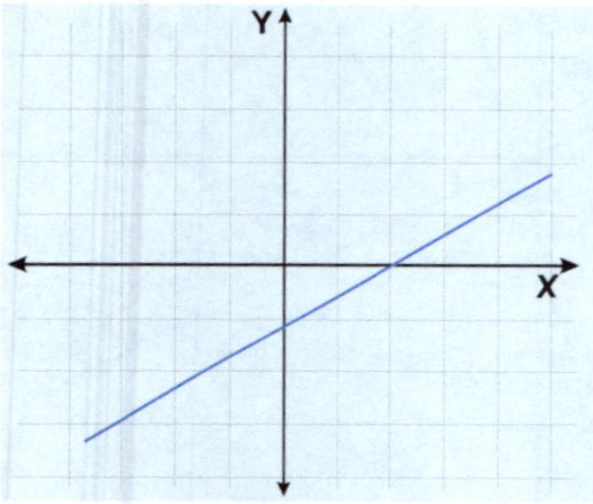

c)

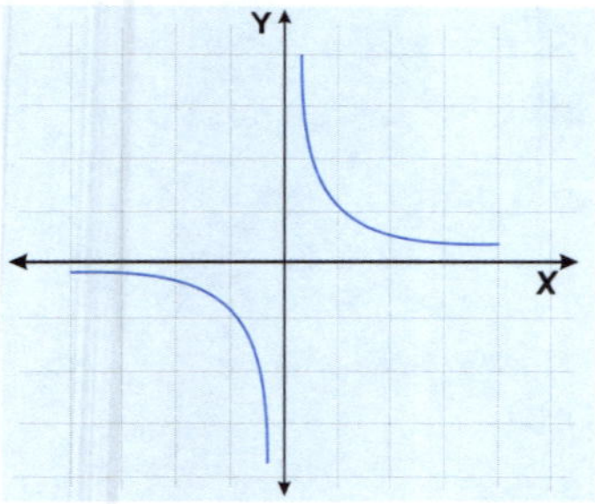

d)

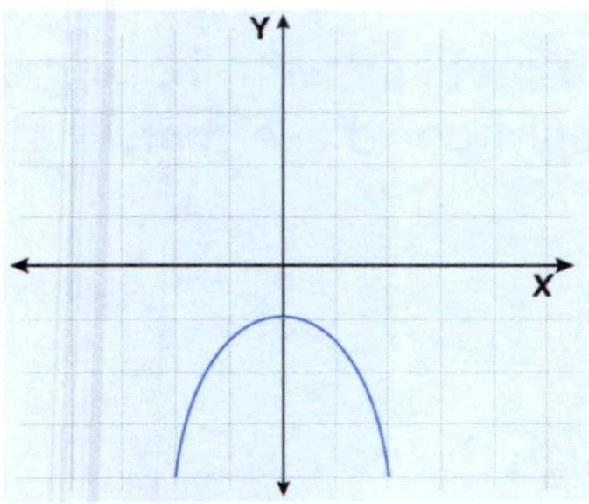

e)

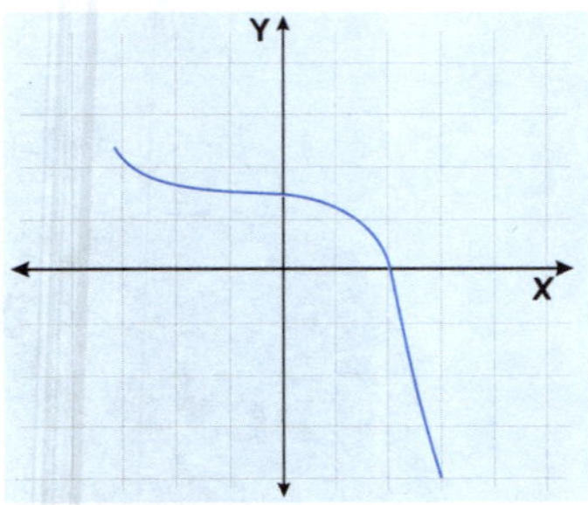

f)

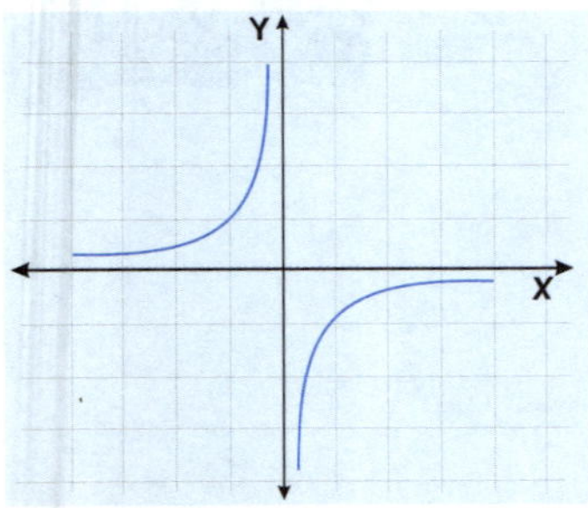

g)

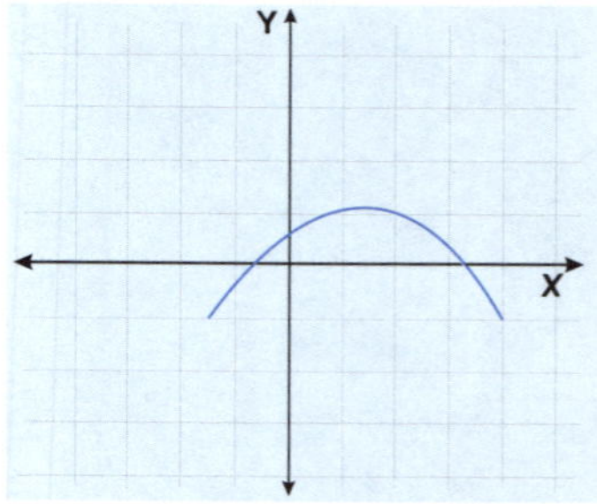

h)

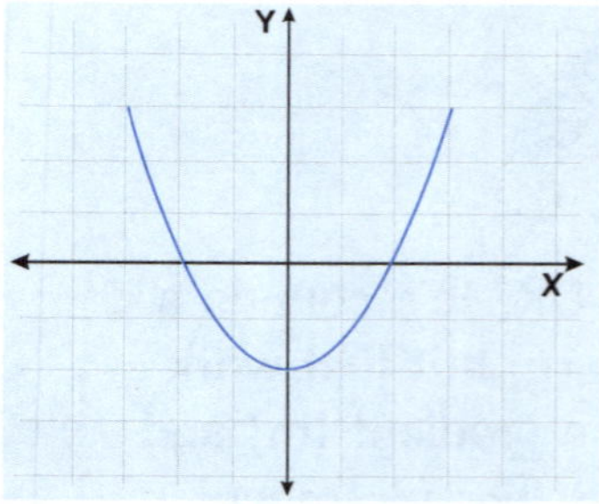

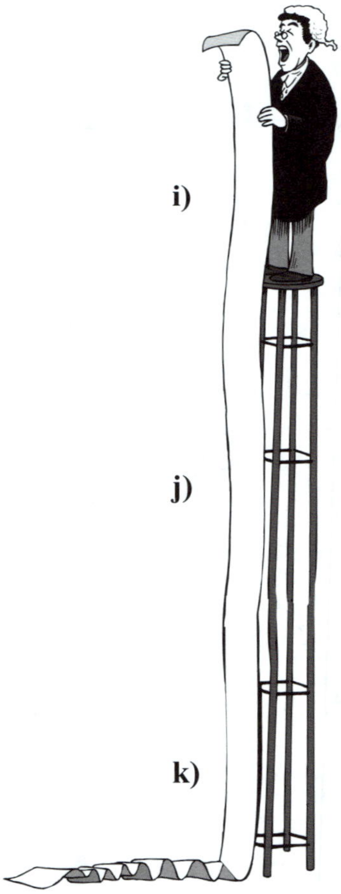

i)

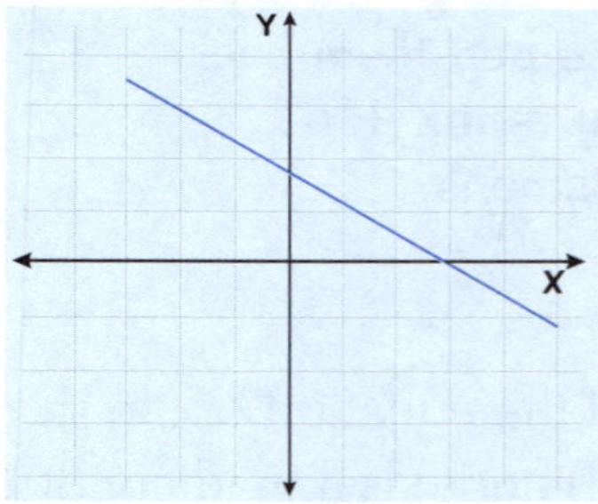

j)

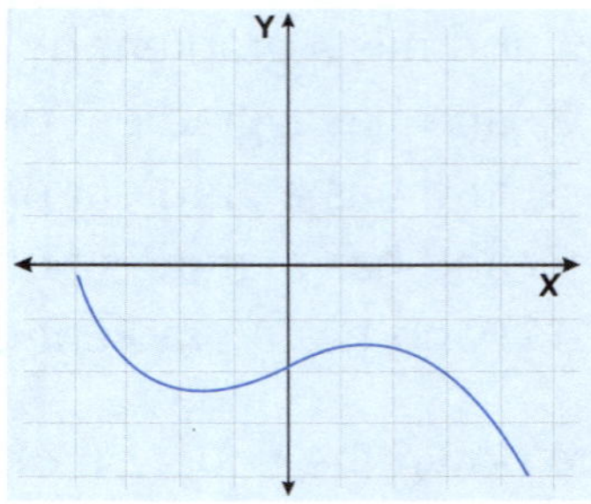

k)

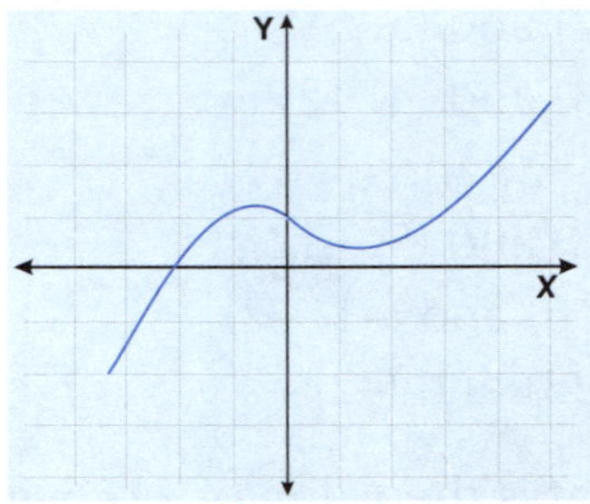

l)

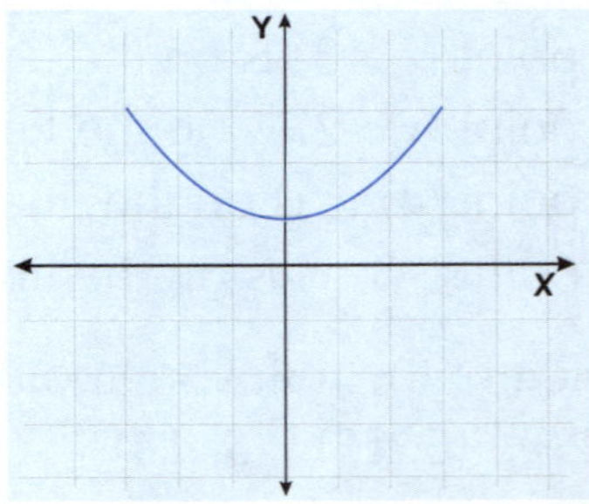

Graphs to Recognise

Q2 Here are some equations, and there are some curves below. Match the equations to the curves on this page and the following page.

a) $y = 3x + 1$

b) $y = 4x - 1$

c) $y = -2x - 1$

d) $y = 3^x$

e) $y = -2x$

f) $y = 3x$

g) $y = -x^2$

h) $y = x^2 + 2$

i) $y = x^2 - 3$

j) $y = -x^2 + 3$

k) $y = -x^2 - 3$

l) $y = x^2$

m) $y = x^3 + 3$

n) $y = 2x^3 - 3$

o) $y = -\frac{1}{2}x^3 + 2$

p) $y = -x^3 + 3$

q) $y = x^3$

r) $y = -\frac{3}{x}$

s) $y = \frac{2}{x}$

t) $y = \frac{1}{x^2}$

u) $y = -\frac{1}{x^2}$

i)

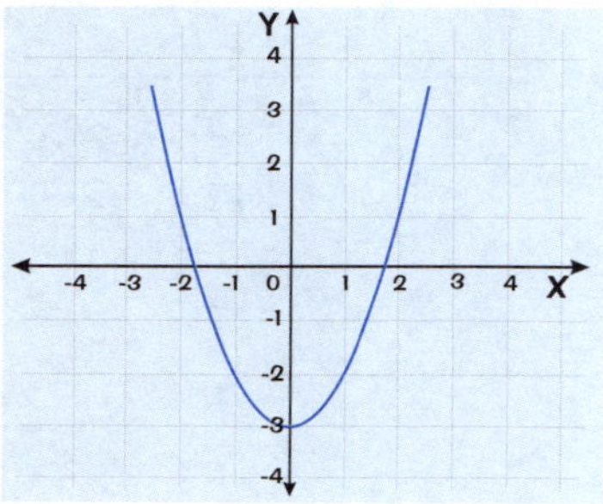

ii)

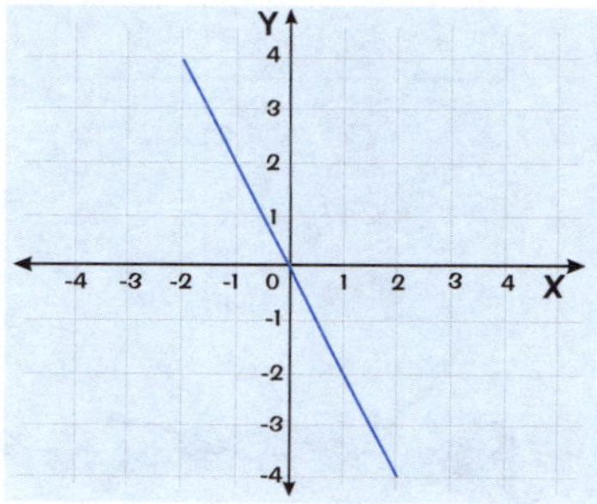

iii)

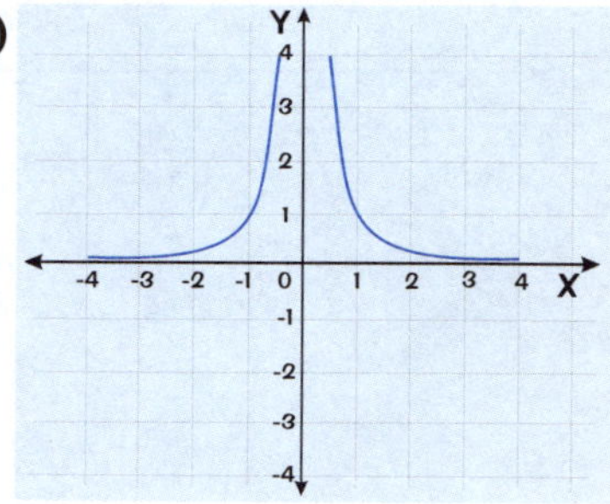

iv)

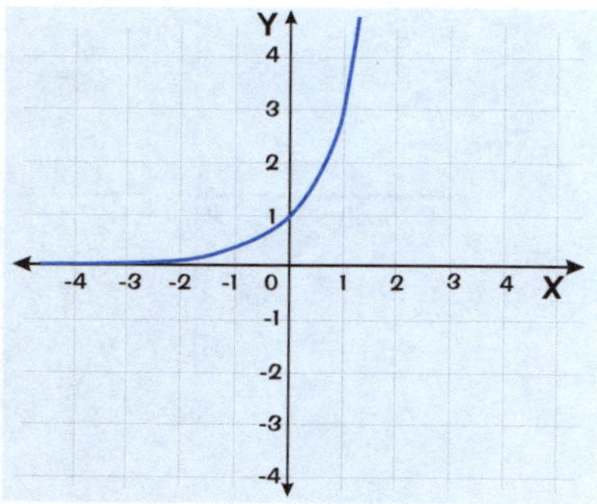

v)

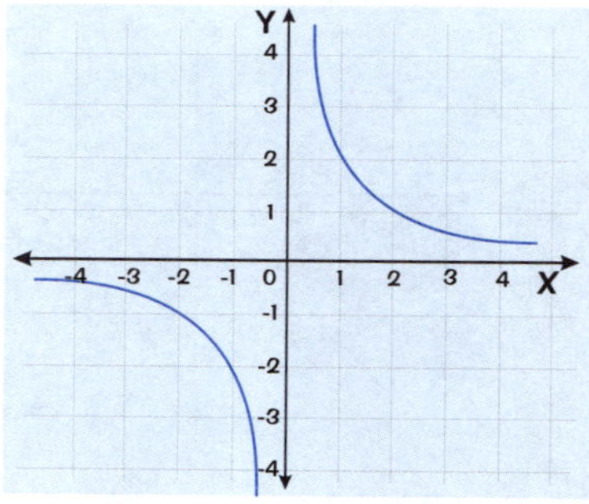

vi)

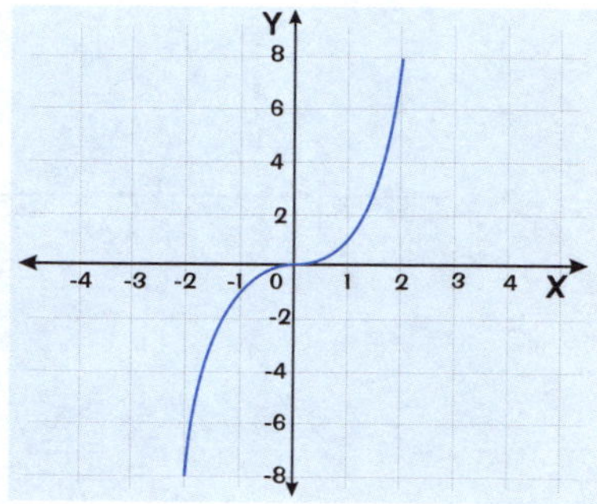

vii)

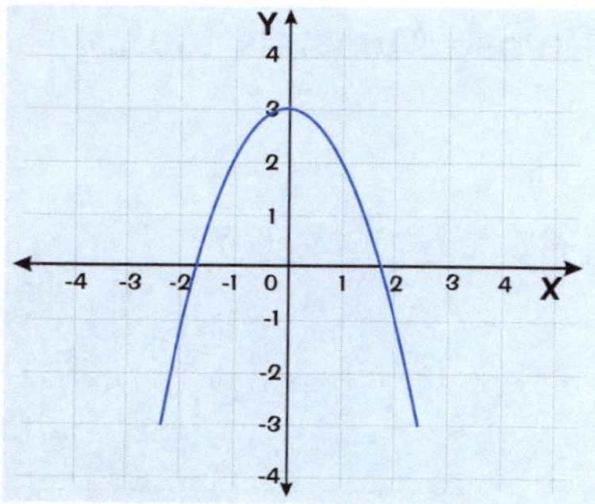

viii)

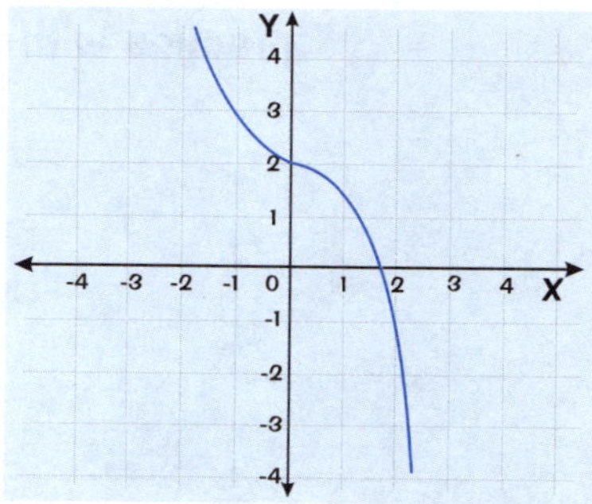

ix)

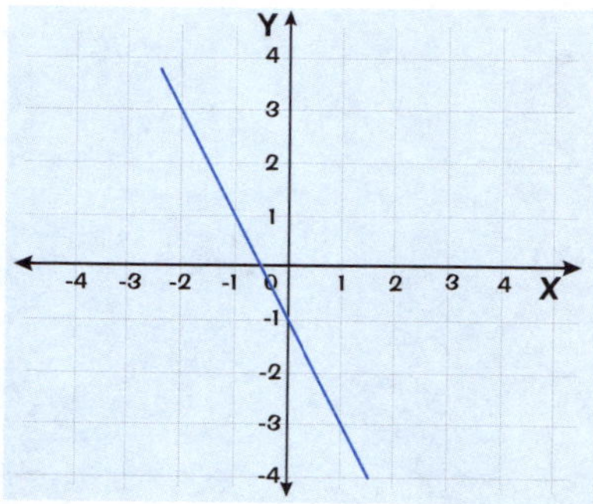

You'll need to be able to sketch a graph from memory — yeah, scary huh. Don't worry — they only expect you to remember the 5 main ones (phew) — straight line (easy), x^2 (buckets), x^3 (wiggly), $1/x$ (2 bits and "x = 0" missing) and k^x (that tricky curve up through (0, 1)).

Graphs to Recognise

x)

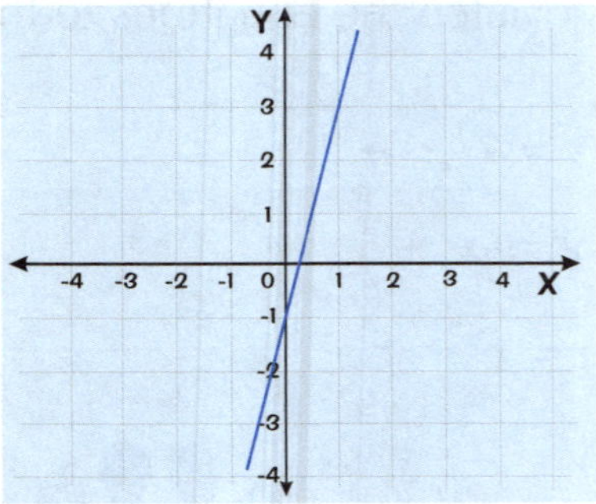

xi)

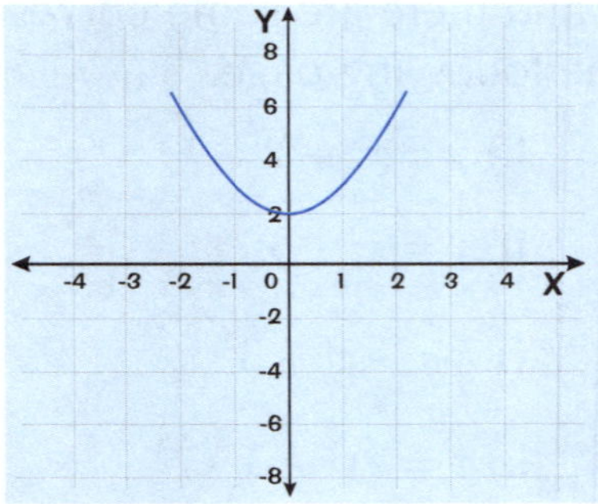

xii)

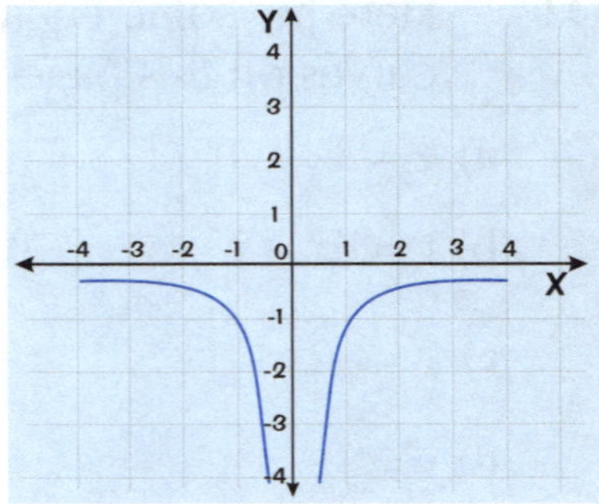

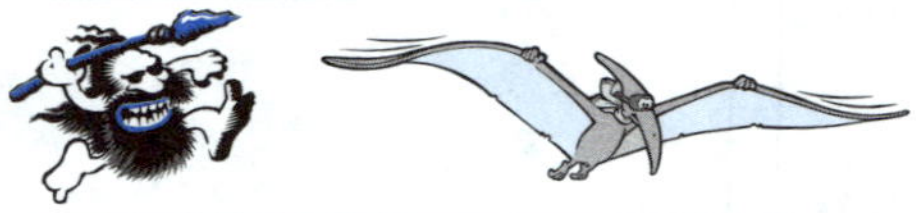

xiii)

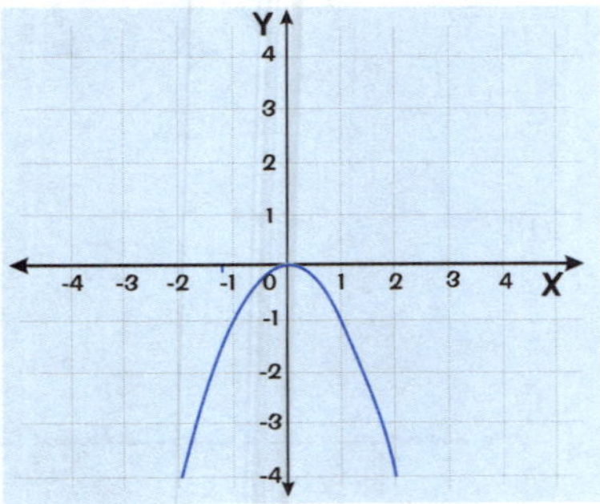

xiv)

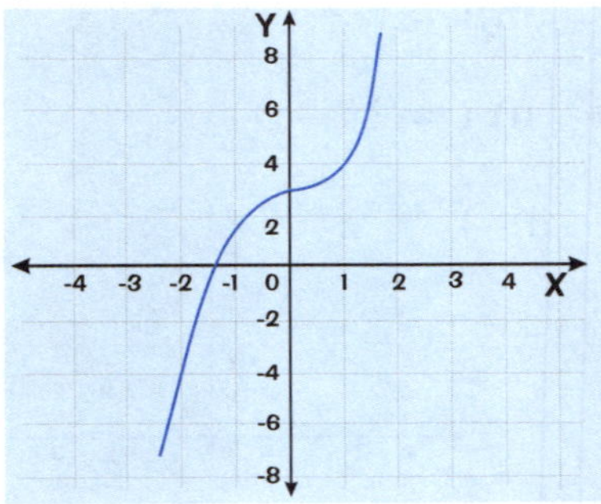

xv)

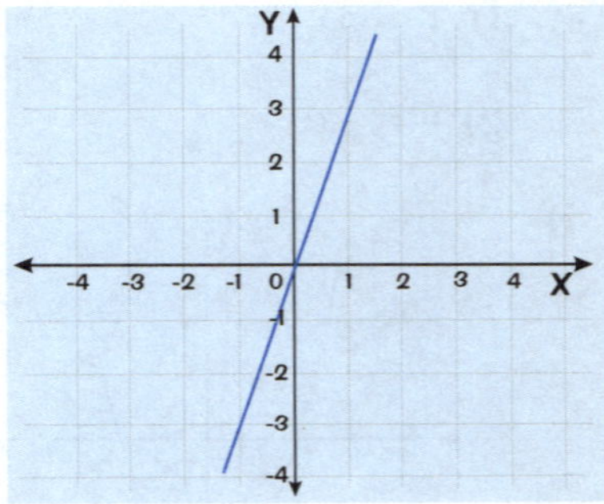

xvi)

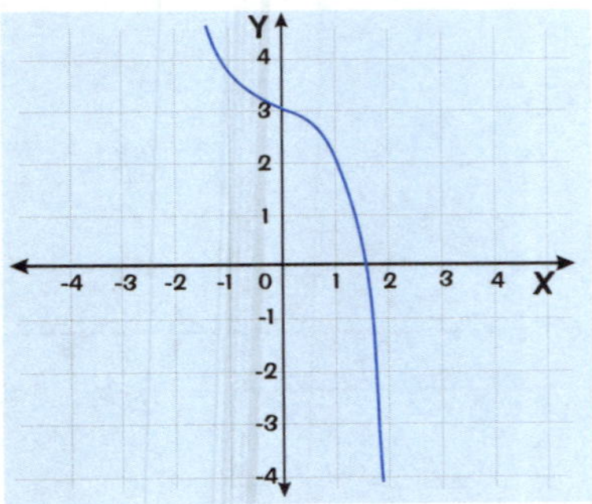

xvii)

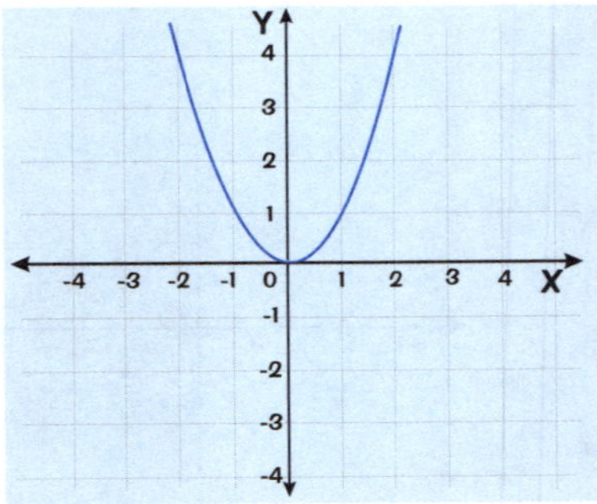

xviii)

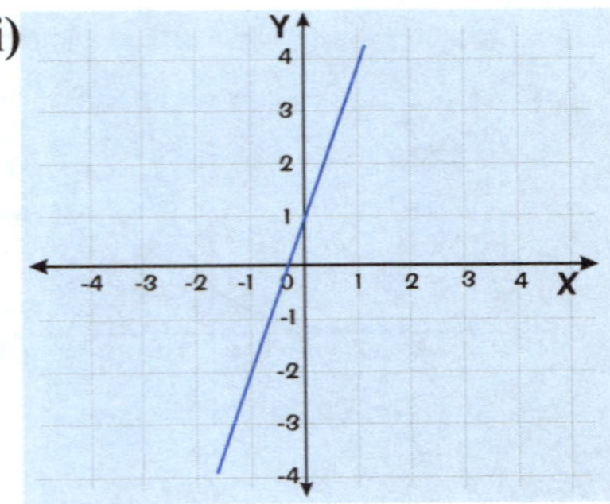

And for an added bonus — there's some practice with your Roman Numerals too...

xix)

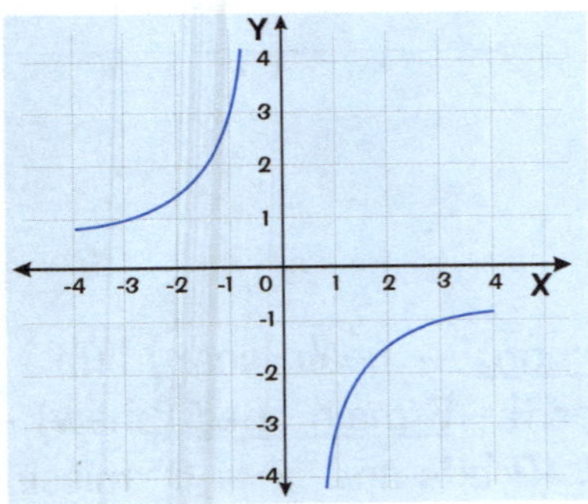

xx)

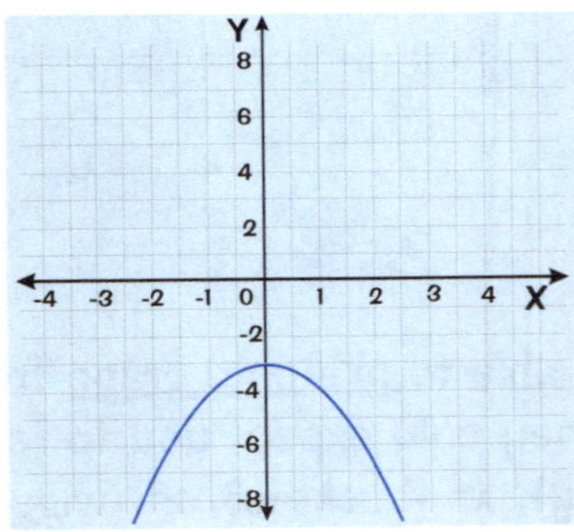

xxi)

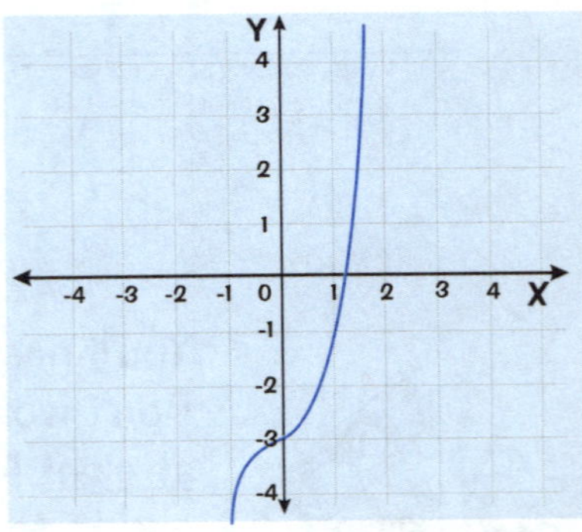

Equations from Graphs

Make sure you know what the four main curves look like, and what their equations are — then you've just got to find the two unknowns and stick 'em back in.

Q1 The table shows the price of electricity.

Number of units used	100	200	300	500
Price (£)	8	11	14	20

Plot the points on a graph with the number of units used on the horizontal axis and the price (£) on the vertical axis.

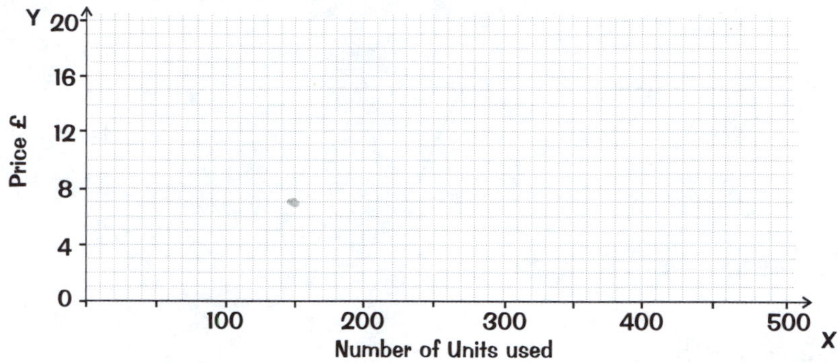

a) Find a formula connecting the price (P) and the number of units (N) used.

b) Use your formula to calculate the price of:

i) 400 units

ii) 700 units.

Q2 Two variables x and y are connected by the equation $y = mx + c$.
Draw a graph with x on the horizontal axis and y on the vertical axis. Use your graph to find the value of:

x	1	3	5	8
y	9	17	25	37

a) m

b) c

— and hence:

c) write down the equation connecting x and y.

d) Use your equation to find the value of y when:

i) $x = 6$

ii) $x = 10$

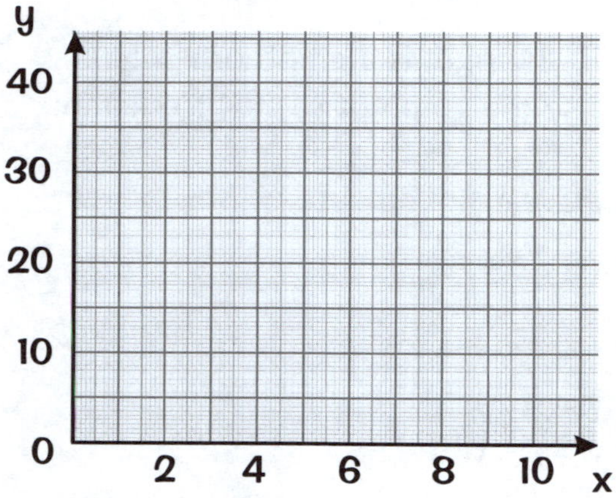

Q3 Two variables A and B are connected by the equation $A = mB^2 + c$.
The table shows some values of A and B.
Choose suitable scales and draw a graph plotting B on the horizontal axis and A on the vertical axis.

B	1	2	3	4
A	10.25	11	12.25	14

a) Use your graph to find: **i)** the value of c **ii)** the value of m

b) Write down the equation connecting A and B

Q4 Two variables C and D are connected by the equation $C = aD^3 + b$.
The table shows some values of C and D.
Choose suitable scales and draw a graph plotting D on the horizontal axis and C on the vertical axis.

D	1	2	2.5	3
C	-4	3	10.625	22

a) Use your graph to find: **i)** the value of b **ii)** the value of a

b) Write down the equation connecting C and D

Transforming Graphs

Q1 This is a graph of $y = f(x)$:

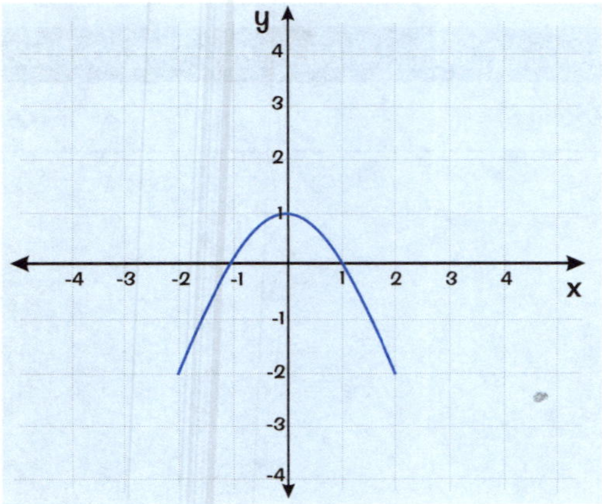

Use the graph of $y = f(x)$ to sketch:

a) $y = f(x) + 3$
b) $y = f(x) - 3$
c) $y = f(x + 3)$
d) $y = f(x - 3)$
e) $y = -f(x)$
f) $y = f(2x)$
g) $y = f(\frac{1}{2}x)$
h) $y = -f(2x)$

You've got to learn about these <u>shifts</u> and <u>stretches</u> — there are <u>only 4</u>, so it won't take long. If you don't, either you'll have to <u>spend ages</u> working it out, or worse still you'll <u>have to guess</u>. Seems a bit of a waste of time <u>and marks</u> to me...

Q2 To the right is a graph of $y = f(x)$.
Use the graph of $y = f(x)$ to sketch:

a) $y = f(x) + 2$
b) $y = f(x) - 2$
c) $y = f(x + 2)$
d) $y = f(x - 2)$
e) $y = -f(x)$
f) $y = f(2x)$
g) $y = f(\frac{1}{2}x)$
h) $y = f(x + 3) - 1$
i) $y = f(x - 1) + 3$

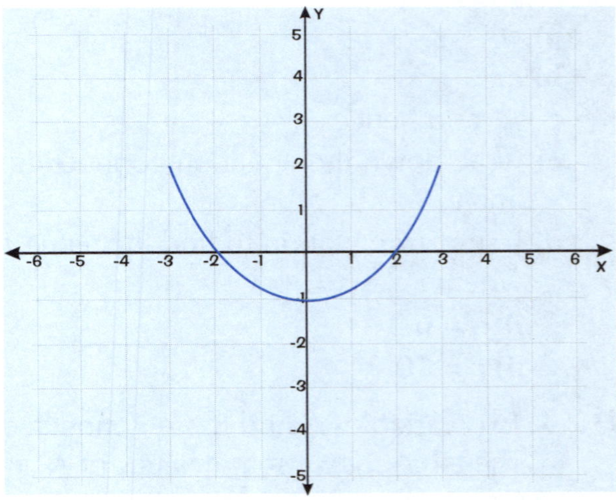

Q3 This is the graph of $y = \cos(x)$:

Sketch the graph of:

a) $y = 2\cos(x)$
b) $y = \cos(2x)$.

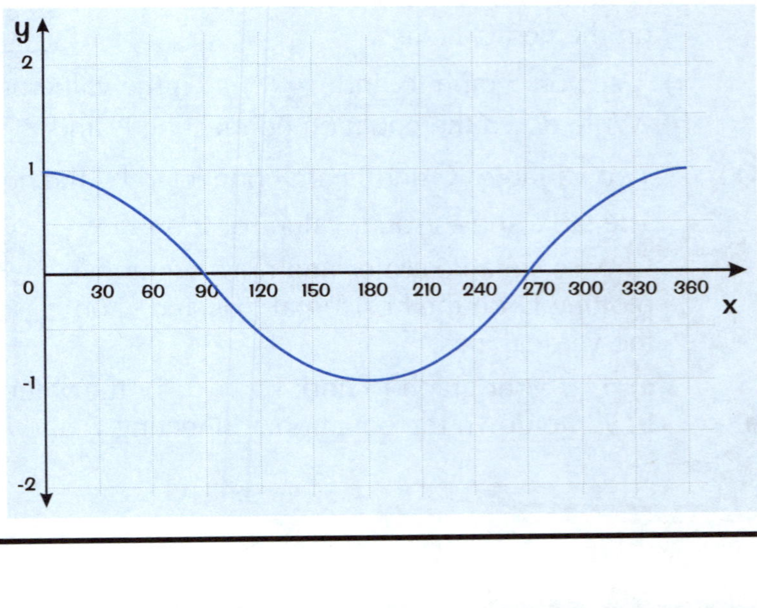

D/T Graphs and V/T Graphs

You need to remember what the different bits of a travel graph mean — what it looks like when stopped, changing speed and coming back to the starting point.

Q1 Peter set out from A at 0900 to walk to B, as shown.

a) How far did he walk in the 1st hour?

b) He stopped twice; how long was each stop?

c) What was his speed after the second stop?

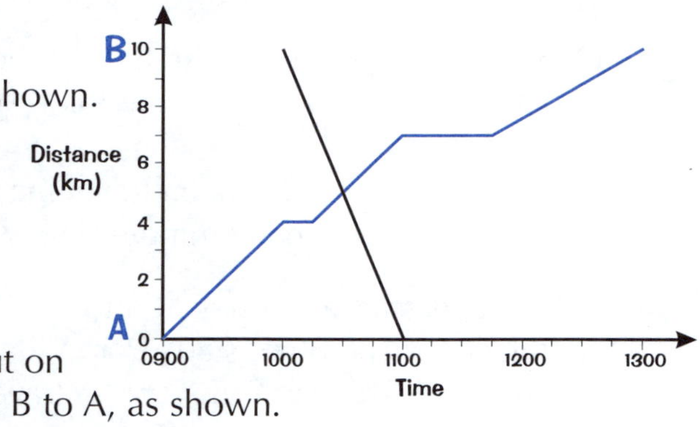

At 1000 Sarah set out on her bike to ride from B to A, as shown.

d) What time did she arrive at A?

e) What was her average speed?

f) At what time did Peter and Sarah pass each other?

Q2 Mr. Smith leaves home at 0730 to go to work. He walks at a steady 6 km/h for 2 km. He catches the 0755 train which takes 35 mins to travel 50 km. He then walks 3 km (at 6 km/h again) to work and arrives at 0900. Draw a graph to show this. How long did he wait at the station for the train?

Q3 The graph on the right shows a return bus journey between Kendal and Sedbergh.

a) How long was the first stop?

b) How long was the second stop?

c) How far did it travel in the first 10 mins?

d) What was the average speed for the journey from Sedbergh to Kendal?

e) What was its fastest speed?

f) What was the average speed for the whole journey?

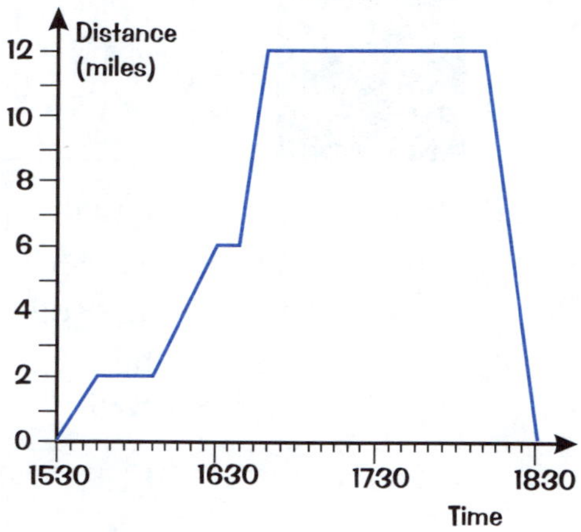

Q4 On sports day the first three in the 1000 m race ran as shown below.

a) Which runner A, B or C won the race?

b) How long did the winner take?

c) Which runner kept up a steady speed?

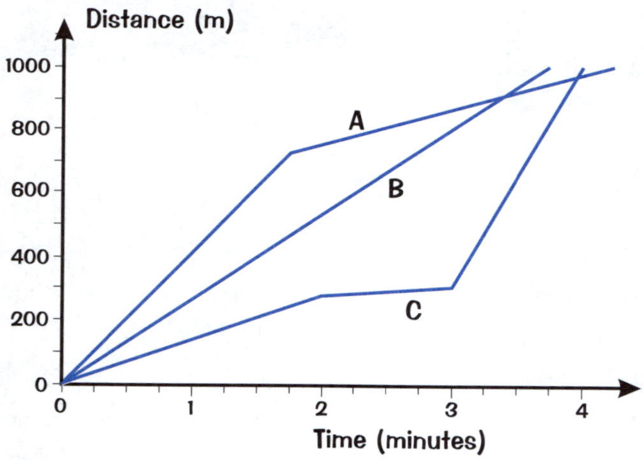

d) What was that speed

i) in m/min?

ii) in km/h?

e) Which runner achieved the fastest speed and what was that speed?

D/T Graphs and V/T Graphs

Q5 This diagram shows the different times taken by 5 trains to travel 100 km.

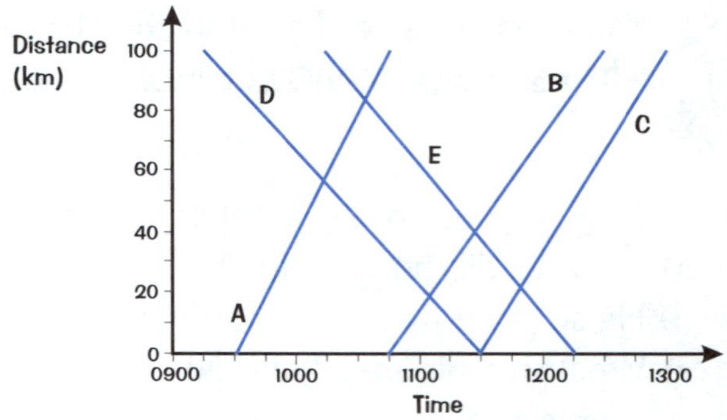

a) Calculate the speed of each train.

b) How could you tell by looking at the diagram which was the fastest and which was the slowest?

c) Train D should have been travelling at 50 km/h. How many minutes late was it?

Q6 Two cars start a journey at midday (1200). One starts from Town A and drives towards Village B. The other starts from Village B and drives towards Town A. A and B are 80 km apart. The car from Town A travels at an average speed of 48 km/h and the other car, from Village B, at 60 km/h.

a) Draw a graph to show these journeys.

b) At what time do the cars pass? (approx.)

c) Approximately how far from A are they when they pass?

Q7 A plane flies from P to Q and after refuelling flies on to R. The table gives the flight details.

Time from P (hrs)	0	1	2	3	4	5	6
Distance from P (km)	0	900	1800	2700	2700	3400	4100

a) Draw a graph to show this journey.

b) What was the average speed from P to Q?

c) What was the average speed from Q to R?

d) At what time was the plane 2000 km from P if it left at 0825?

Remember that the gradient of the graph is the speed. When you're drawing these graphs, make sure you choose sensible units for your axes, and when you read off the answer, remember to use those units. Don't just measure it in cm!

Q8 A girl sets off on an all-day walk. She started at 0915 and walked at a steady speed for 9 km before stopping at 1100 for a 20 min break. She then set off again at a steady speed and walked 8 km, stopping at 1300 for 45 mins. After lunch she walked at $3\frac{1}{2}$ km/h for $2\frac{1}{2}$ hrs to her destination.

a) Draw a graph to show this walk.

b) How far did she walk altogether?

c) What was the average speed for the whole walk?

d) What was her fastest walking speed?

Q9 The graph on the right shows a car journey.

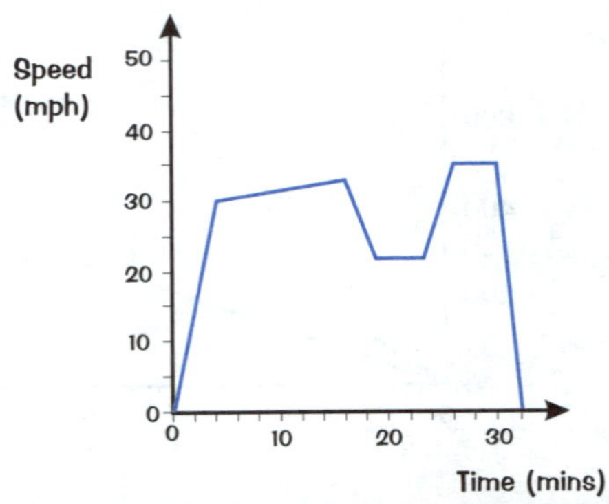

a) How long did the journey last?

b) How often did it travel at a steady speed?

c) For how many minutes was it travelling over 30 mph?

d) During which times was the acceleration greatest?

e) How long did it take to slow down at the end?

f) What was the fastest speed achieved?

D/T Graphs and V/T Graphs

Don't worry — there's nothing too tricky in here and they're all pretty much the same — if you can do one, you can do them all.

Q10 The diagram opposite shows how a cyclist rode part of a race. Calculate:

a) the acceleration between 0 and 10 mins
b) the deceleration between 20 and 25 mins
c) the total distance travelled in 35 mins
d) the average speed for the first 30 mins.

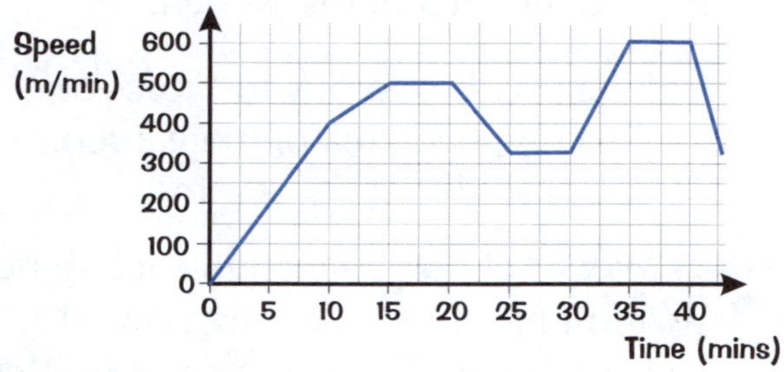

Q11 A car accelerates steadily from rest to a speed of 100 km/h, taking 25 seconds to do this.

a) Draw a speed/time graph to show this.
b) Calculate the total distance covered.

Q12 Two vehicles start from rest at the same time. One accelerates steadily at a rate of 0.65 m/sec^2. The other accelerates as shown in the table.

Time (seconds)	0	2	4	6	8	10	12	14
Speed (m/s)	0	1	1.5	2.3	3.2	5.5	7.8	10

a) Draw these speed/time graphs on the same axes.
b) Estimate when both vehicles are travelling at the same speed.
c) Is there any difference in the distance travelled by each?

Q13 This is a speed-time graph of a train journey:

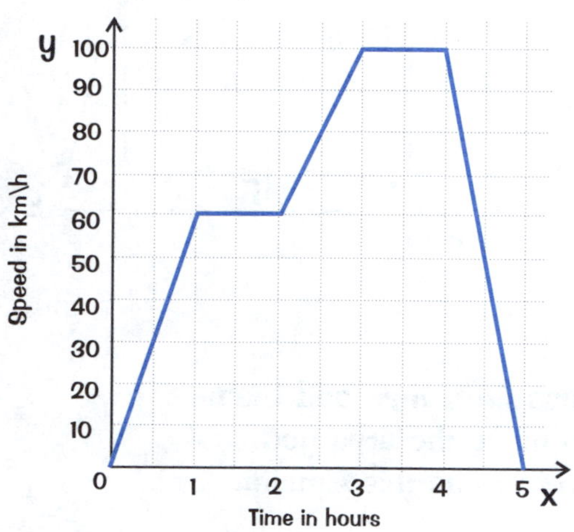

a) Calculate the distance travelled in:
i) The first two hours.
ii) The last two hours.
b) Calculate the total distance travelled.

Q14 This is a speed-time graph of a cycle ride:

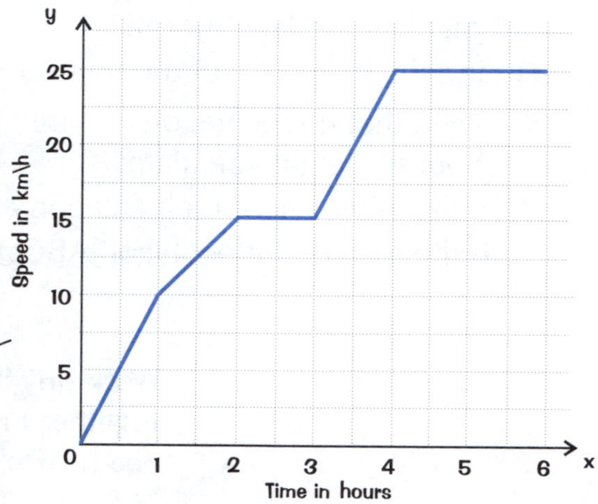

a) Calculate the distance travelled in:
i) The first two hours.
ii) The last two hours.
b) Calculate the total distance travelled.

Add up all the little trapeziums to find the whole area — easy trapeasy...

Areas

Q1 The diagram shows a plan of Julian's garden.

a) Calculate the perimeter of the garden.

b) Find the area of the garden.

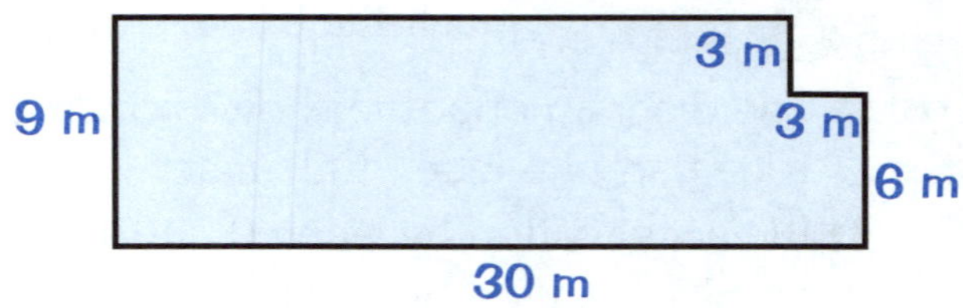

Julian wishes to buy turf to cover the complete area of the garden. Turf is sold in units of 4 m^2.

c) Work out how many units Julian needs to cover the whole garden.

d) Turf costs £7.90 per unit plus £12.50 for delivery. Find the total cost of the turf plus delivery.

Q2 A 45 m length of cooking foil is 45 cm wide. Find the area of foil on the roll in m^2.

Q3 The diagram shows a trapezium ABCD in which DC is parallel to AB.

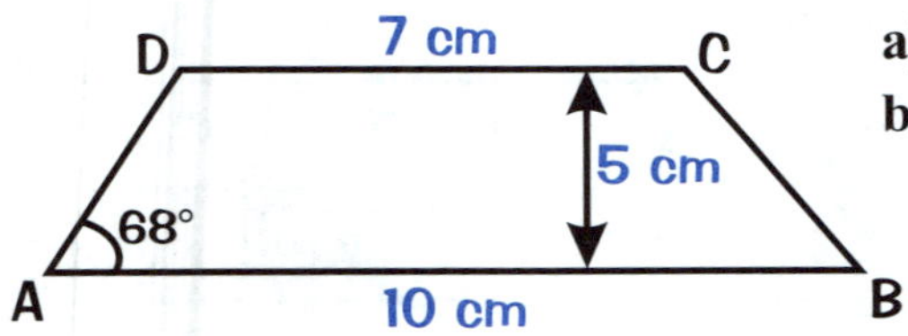

a) Angle BAD = 68°. Find the size of angle ADC.

b) AB = 10 cm. CD = 7 cm. The perpendicular distance between the parallel sides is 5 cm. Calculate the area of the trapezium.

Q4 ABCDE is a pentagon as shown.

a) Length BC = 1.8 m and angle CBG = 20°. Calculate the length of BG.

b) Length AB = 5 m and length AH = 0.8 m. Calculate the length of BH.

c) Find the height CF of the pentagon.

d) Given that the pentagon is symmetrical about its height calculate:

i) the width AE of the pentagon

ii) the area of the pentagon ABCDE.

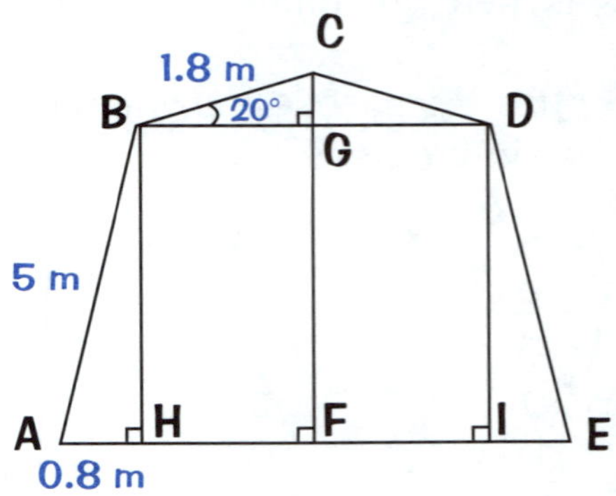

Work out the individual areas first, then add them together or take bits off to make the area you need. If only everything in life was this simple...

Q5 Lengths are denoted by a, b and h. Which formulas represent areas?

a) $\pi(a + b)$

b) $\pi h(a + b)^2$

c) $\pi^2 h$

d) $\pi(a + b)h$

e) $\pi(a + b)h^2$

Remember :—

if r is a length, then r^2 is an area and r^3 is a volume.

Areas

Remember what I said about these tricky area questions — you'll find them quite easy if you split them into simple shapes.

Q6 A playground is to contain a sand pit. It is in the shape of a cylinder of diameter 5 m and height 0.8 m. It must be lined on the bottom and on the walls with plastic sheet. Find:

a) the area of the sand pit which must be lined

b) the number of sheets required if each sheet is sold in the form of rectangles 1.3 m long and 0.5 m wide.

The mass of 1 m^3 of sand is 1.4 tonnes. Find:

c) the volume of sand required in m^3

d) the mass of sand required to the nearest tonne.

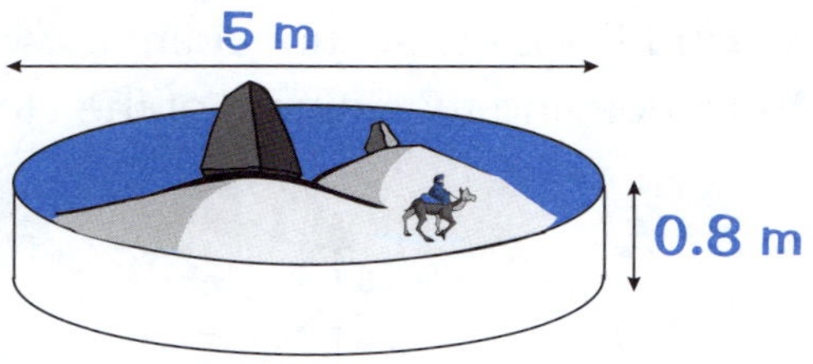

Q7 A plastic strip is made in the shape shown. The curves AC and BD are both arcs of circles with centre O. The larger circle has radius 30 mm and the smaller circle has radius 20 mm. The shaded ends of the shape are both semicircles.

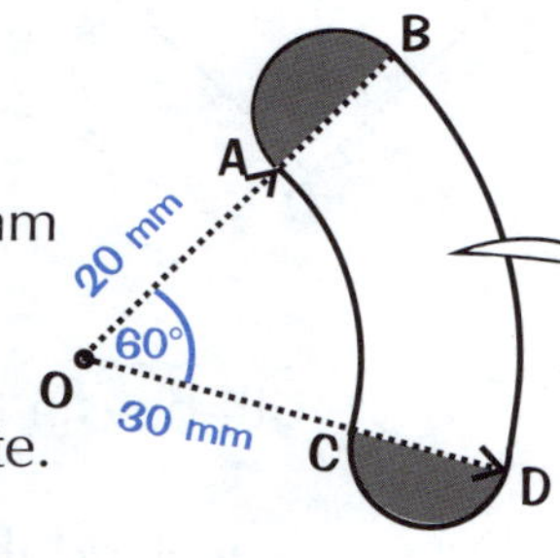

a) Find the area of the shape ABDC, shown in white.

b) Find the area of the two semicircular ends. Hence write down the area of the complete shape.

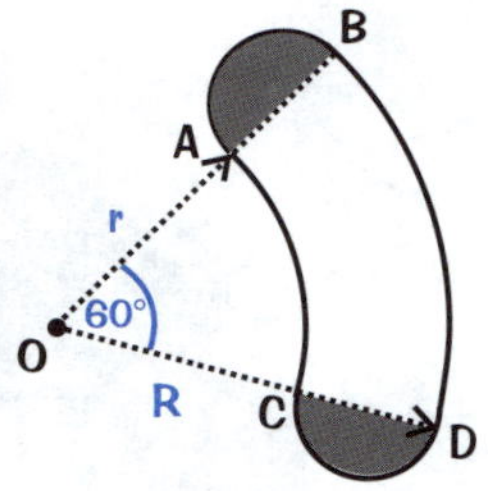

Suppose the radius of the arc AC is now r and that of BD is R.

c) Write down a formula for the area of the sector OBD in terms of R.

d) Write down an expression for the area of the white shape ABDC in terms of r and R.

e) Hence write down an expression for the area of the complete shape.

Q8 ABCD is a field with AB = 100 m, BC = 90 m and CD = 60 m. DE is a fence across the field with EA = x m.

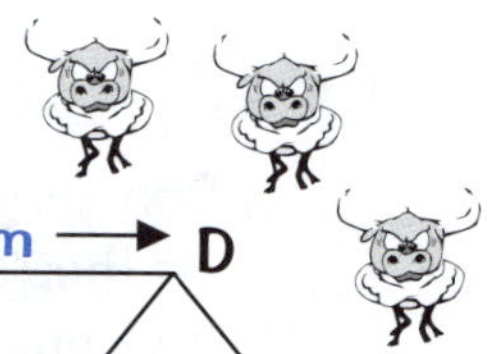

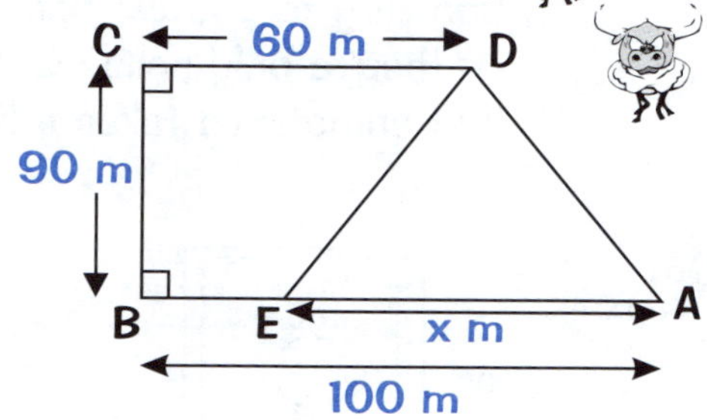

a) Find the area of the field ABCD.

b) Find an expression in terms of x for the area of triangle DEA.

c) The fence DE is arranged so that the ratio of the area of triangle DEA : area of trapezium BEDC = 3:5.

i) Find the value of x for this ratio.

ii) Write down the area of triangle DEA using the value of x found in **i)**.

Volumes

Make sure you know the 4 main volume formulas — spheres, prisms, pyramids, cones.

Q1 a, b and h are lengths. Which of the following formulas could represent a volume? Give a reason for your answer.

a) πabh
b) $\pi(a + b)h$
c) $\pi h^2(a + b)$
d) $\pi h^2(a + b)^2$

Q2 Joe buys a garden cloche to protect his plants from frost. It has a semicircular diameter of 70 cm and a length of 3 m.

a) Find the cross-sectional area.
b) Hence find the volume of the cloche.

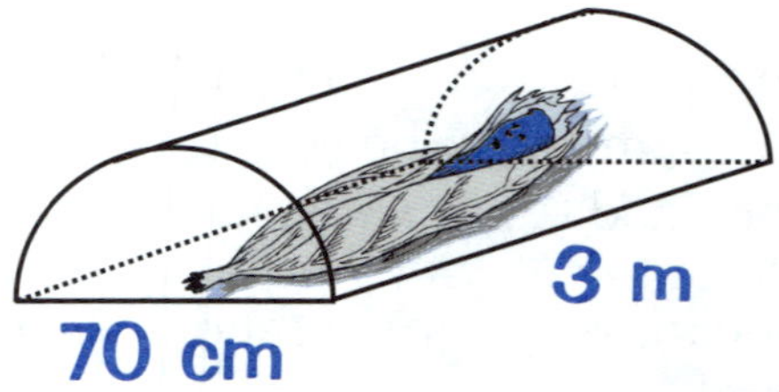

Q3

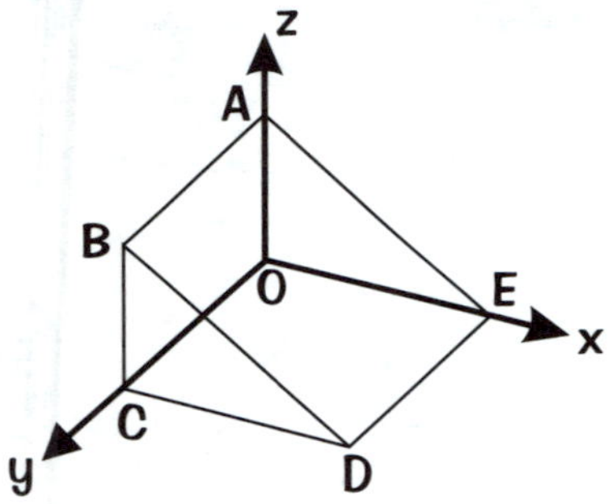

The diagram shows a triangular prism.
The coordinates of A are (0, 0, 5).
The coordinates of E are (4, 0, 0).
The coordinates of C are (0, 8, 0).

a) Write down the coordinates of:
i) B
ii) D.
b) Calculate the volume of the prism.

Q4

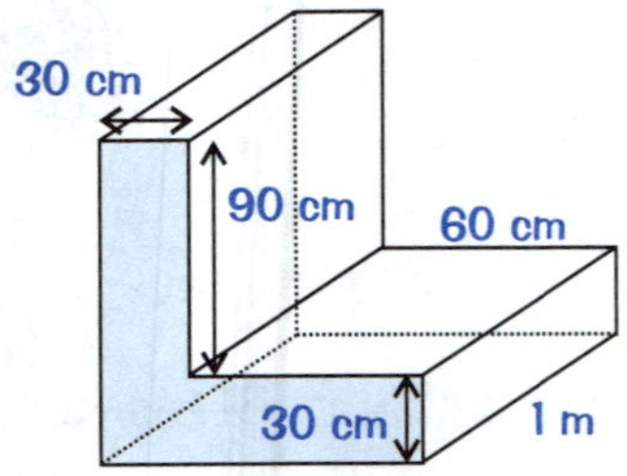

Jill buys a bookshelf with the dimensions shown in the diagram.

a) Find the cross-sectional area, shown in pink.
b) Find the volume of the bookshelf in m^3.

Q5 Busy Buses Ltd decide to put a bus shelter near their main town-centre stop. It has the dimensions shown.

a) Find the area of the cross-section of the shelter.
b) Find the volume of the bus shelter.

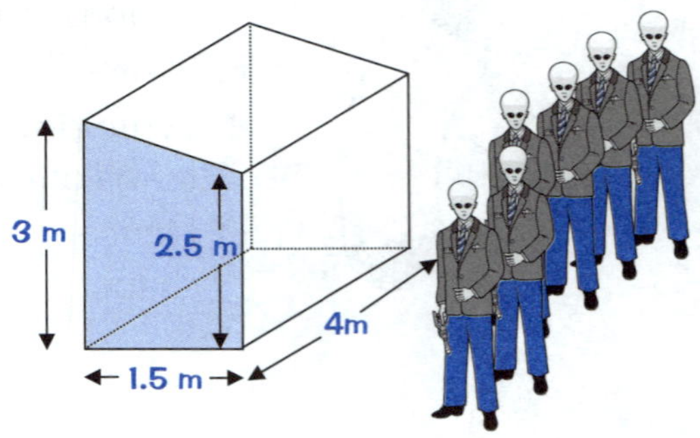

Contrary to popular belief, there isn't anything that complicated about prisms — they're only solids with the same shape all the way through. The only bit that sometimes takes a little longer is finding the cross-sectional area.

Q6

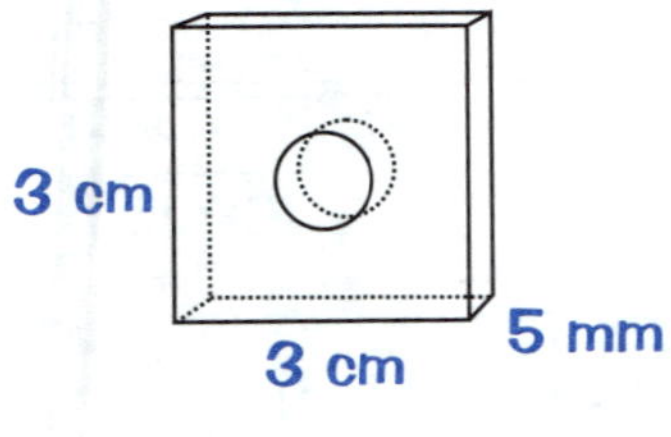

A nut has the cross-section illustrated. The circular hole has a diameter of 1.4 cm and the nut is 5 mm thick.
Find the volume of the nut in cm^3.

Volumes

Q7 Bill bought a new garden shed with dimensions as shown. Find:

a) the area of the cross-section
b) the volume of the shed
c) the length AB
d) the total area of the roof.

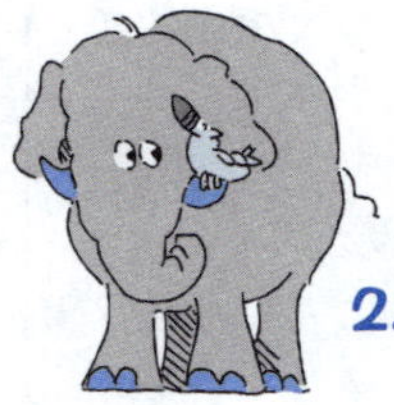

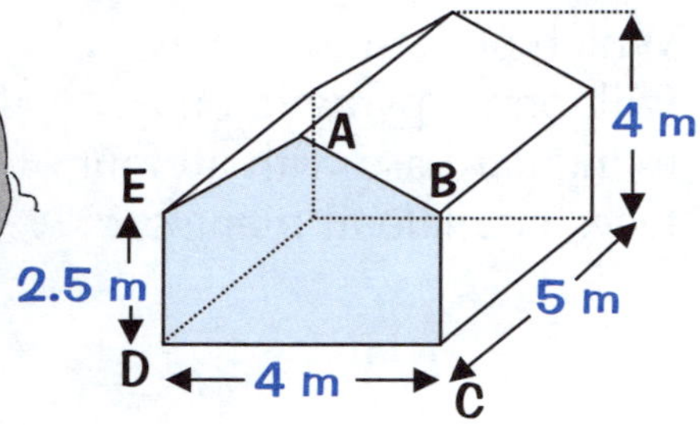

Q8

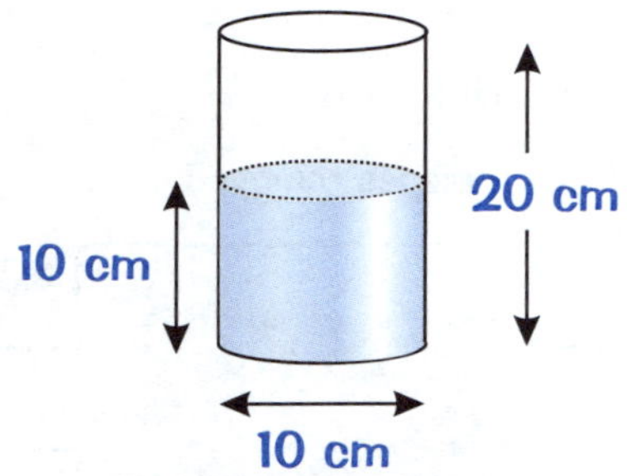

A cylindrical container of diameter 10 cm and height 20 cm is filled with water to a depth of 10 cm. 3200 identical ball bearings are now submerged in the water. The depth increases to 18 cm. Calculate the radius of one ball bearing.

Q9 An egg timer is symmetrical and consists of hemispheres, cylinders and cones joined together as shown.

a) Calculate the volume of sand in the upper container.
Sand runs into the bottom container at a constant rate of 0.05 cm^3 per second.

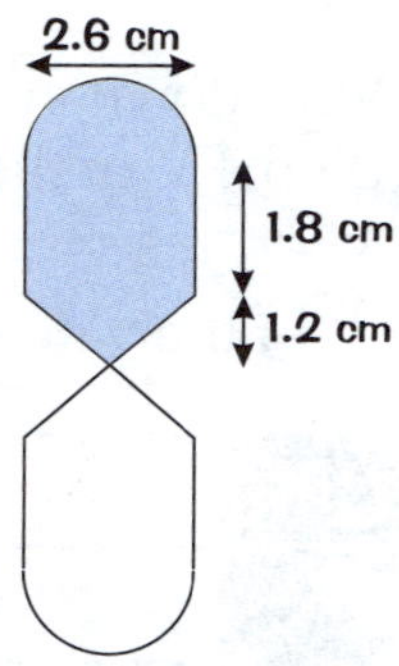

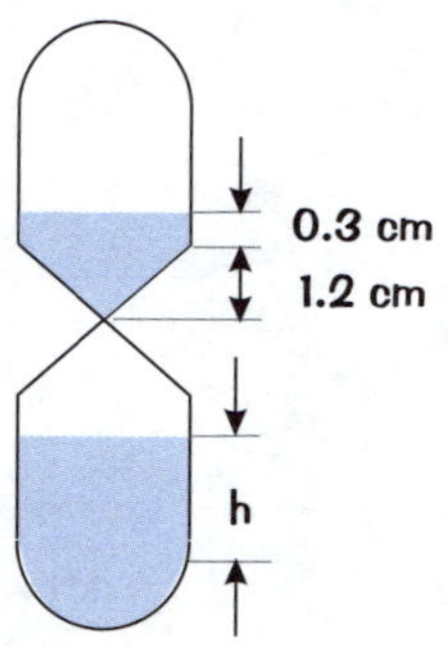

At the end of a certain time period the sand has fallen through into the bottom container as shown.

b) How high (***h***) has it risen up the cylindrical part of the bottom container?

c) How long has it taken the sand to fall through until it is at this height?

Q10 A metal cube, each of whose sides is 10 cm long, is melted down and made into a cylinder 10 cm high. What is the radius of this cylinder?

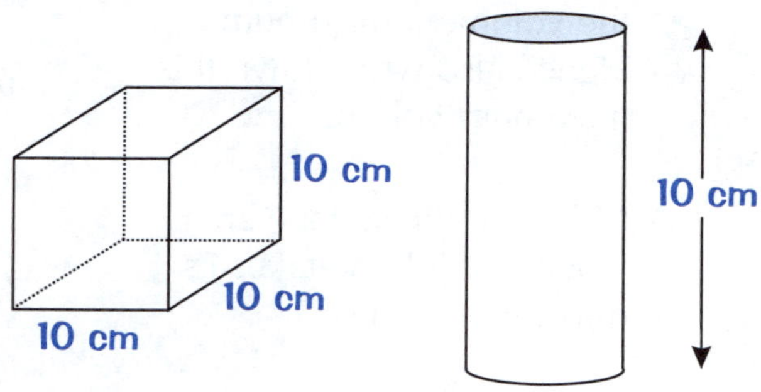

Q11 Water is flowing into each of these containers at a constant rate. For each container, sketch the graph of the depth of water against time.

a)

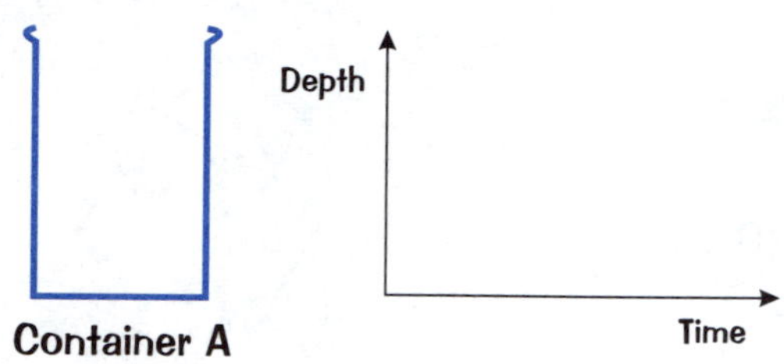

b)

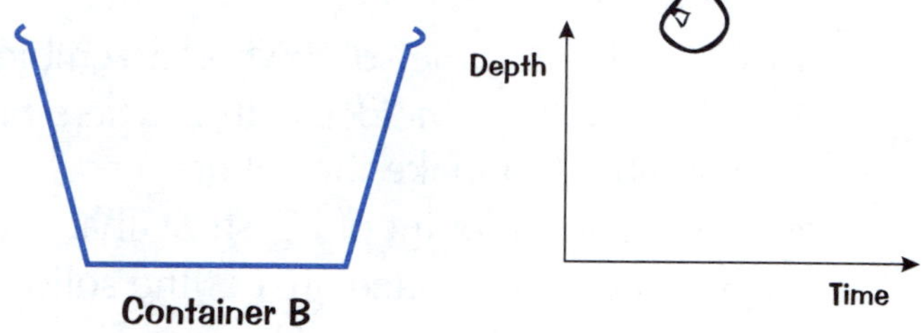

Length, Area and Volume

Q1 Which of these two nets will form a pyramid on a triangular base with all four faces equilateral triangles?

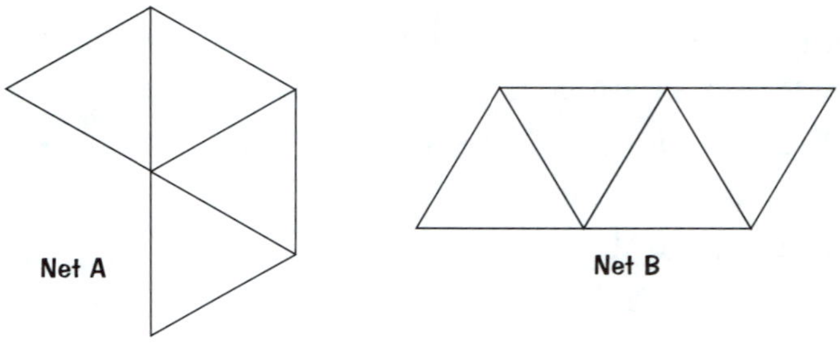

Q2 A net is cut out from a cardboard rectangle as shown in the diagram.

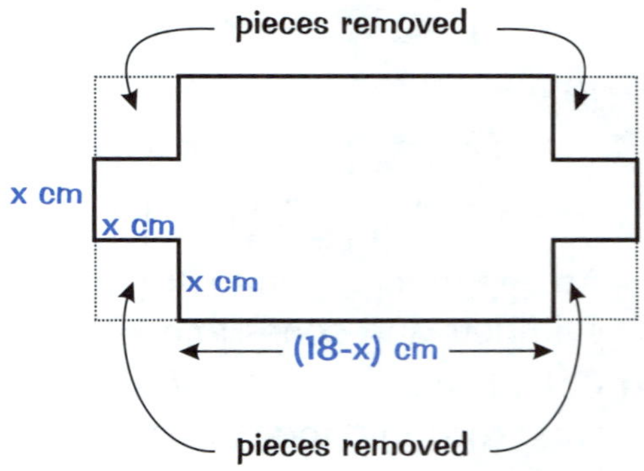

a) Show that the net forms a box with no lid by drawing the solid, adding on all measurements in terms of x.

b) Write down an expression for the volume V of the box in terms of x.

c) Fill in the values of V in this table.

x	8	10	12	14	16
V		800			

d) Draw the graph of V against x.

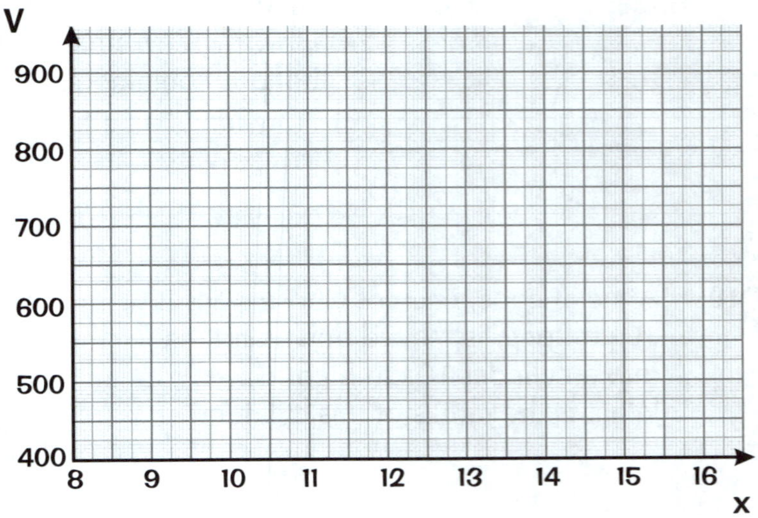

e) Write down from your graph the value of x which makes the volume a maximum. Hence also write down this maximum volume.

f) Calculate the surface area when the volume takes its maximum value.

Q3 The diagram shows the net of a solid. EFGH is a square which forms the base. Triangles ABC, BCD, CDE and CFE are equilateral triangles. Length GH = 6 cm.

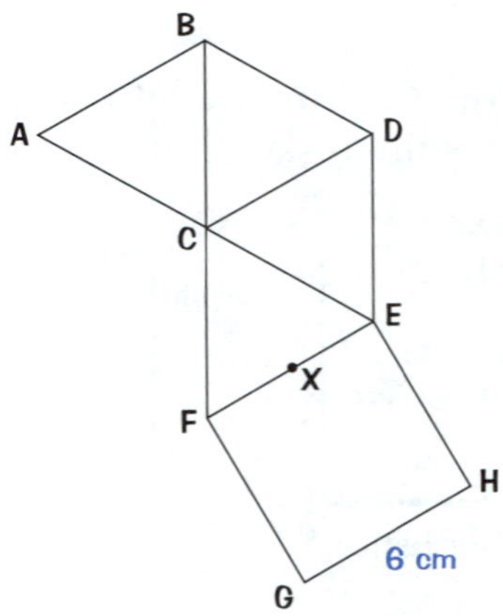

a) What shape is the solid when assembled?

b) Which point coincides with B when the net is assembled to make the solid?

c) If X is the midpoint of FE, show that CX is 5.20 cm.

d) Find the total surface area of the solid.

e) Find the height of the solid.

Circle Geometry

Just when you thought geometry was getting easy... now you've got circles to contend with.

Eeeek.

Q1 ABCD is a cyclic quadrilateral with angle BCD = 100°.
EF is a tangent to the circle touching it at A.
Angle DAF = 30°.
Write down the size of angle:

a) BAD
b) EAB.

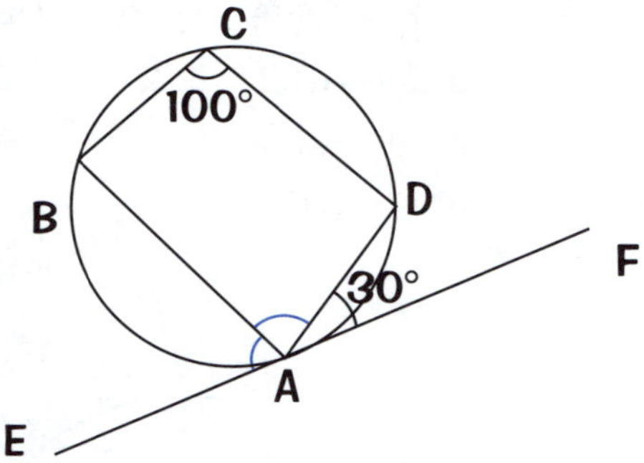

Q2

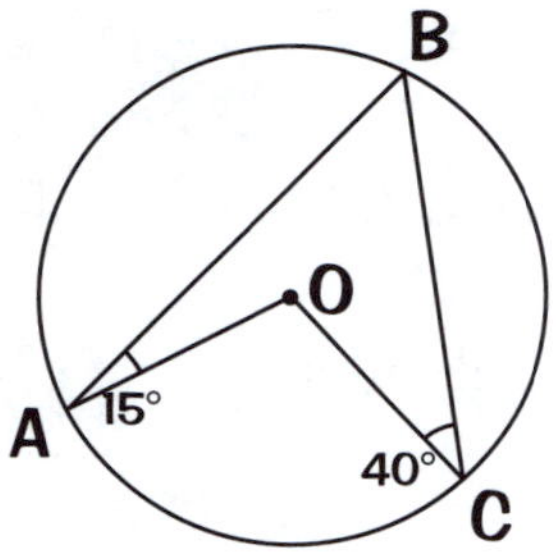

A, B and C are points on the circumference of a circle and O is the centre. Angle BAO = 15° and angle BCO = 40°. Find:

a) angle ABC
b) angle AOC.

Q3 A, B, C, D and E are points on the circumference of a circle, centre O. Angle BDE = 53°. The line AF is a tangent to the circle, touching it at A. Angle EAF = 32°. Find:

a) angle BOE
b) angle ACE.

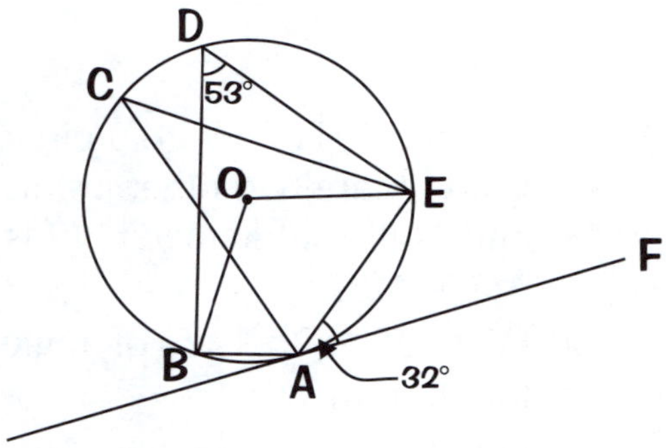

Q4 ABCD is a cyclic quadrilateral and the tangent to the circle at A makes an angle of 70° with the side AD. Angle BCA = 30°. Write down, giving a reason, the size of:

a) angle ACD
b) angle BAD.

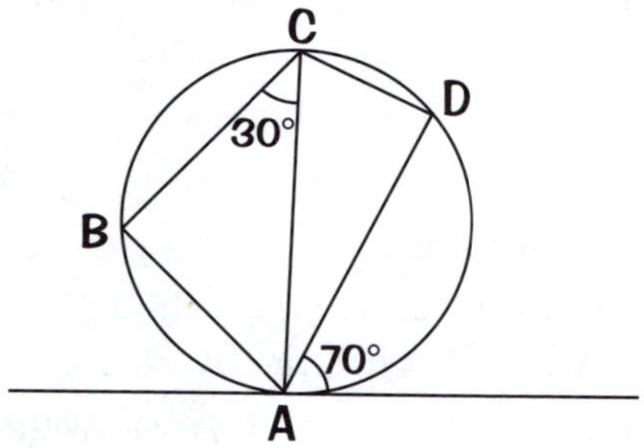

Q5

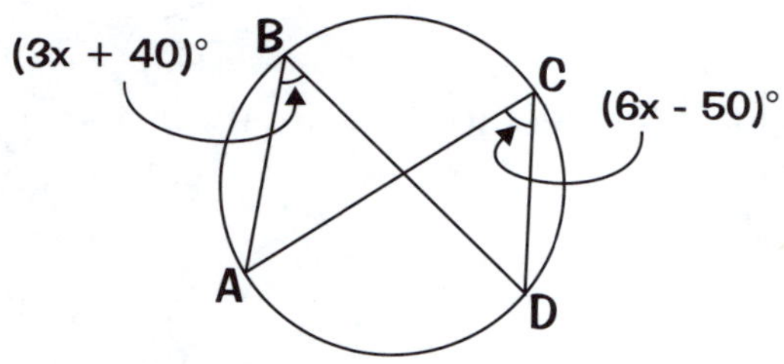

A, B, C and D are points on the circumference of a circle. Angle ABD = $(3x + 40)°$ and angle ACD = $(6x - 50)°$.

a) Give a reason why angle ABD and angle ACD are the same.
b) Form an equation in x and by solving it, find the size of angle ABD.

Q6 A circle, centre O, has radius OA = 5 cm. Angle OAB = 40°. Calculate the length of the chord AB.

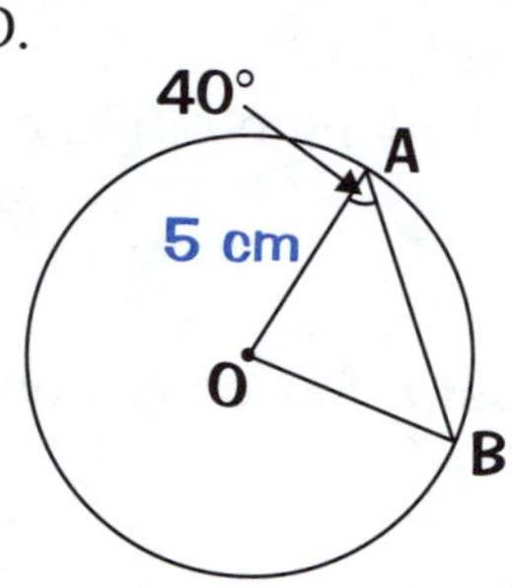

Beware the sneaky isosceles...

Circle Geometry

Q7 A, B, C and D are points on the circumference of a circle. O is the centre of the circle and angle AOD = 140°. Write down:

a) angle ABD

b) angle ABC

c) angle DBC.

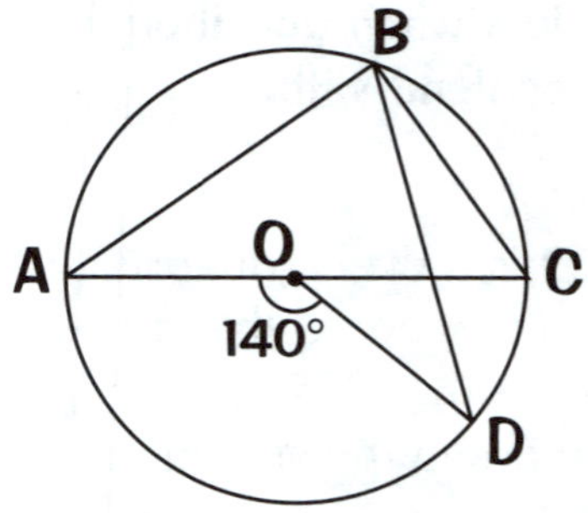

Q8

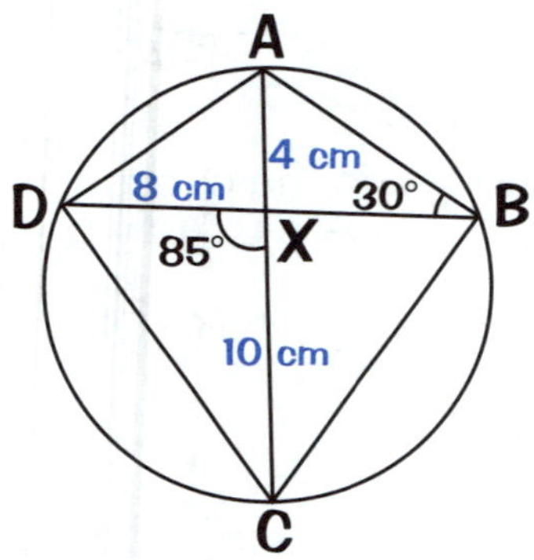

ABCD is a cyclic quadrilateral. The lines AC and BD intersect at X. Lengths AX = 4 cm, DX = 8 cm and XC = 10 cm. Angles DXC = 85° and ABD = 30°.

a) Show that triangles DXC and AXB are similar.

b) Find the length of XB.

c) Write down the size of angle BDC.

Q9 A tangent is drawn to a circle touching it at A. C and B are two other points on the circumference and AOB is a diameter. O is the centre of the circle. Angle ABC is 23°.

a) Write down the size of angle ACB, giving a reason for your answer.

b) Find the size of the angle marked $x°$ in the diagram.

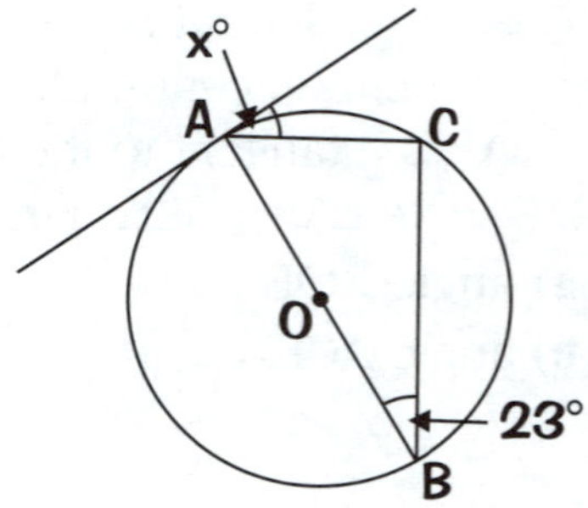

Q10 B, C and D are three points on the circumference of a circle with BD as a diameter. O is the centre of the circle and ADC is a straight line. AB = 10 cm and BC = 3 cm.

a) Write down the size of angle ACB. Give a reason for your answer.

b) Show that AC is 9.54 cm correct to 2 decimal places.

c) If AD = 5 cm, find the length of the diameter DOB correct to 2 decimal places.

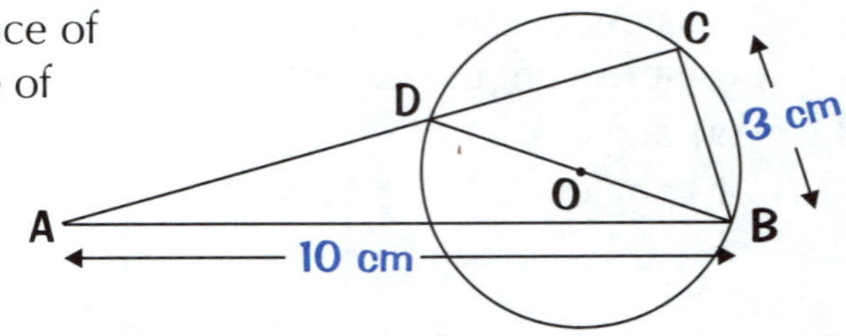

Q11 O is the centre of a circle and AB is a chord. The length OA = 5 cm and angle OAB = 20°. Find the length of the chord AB.

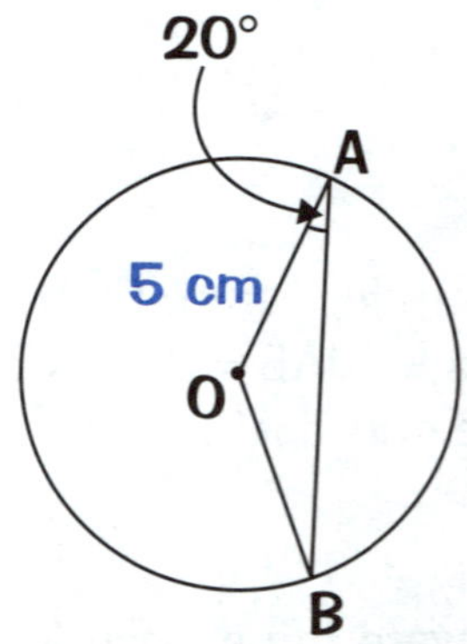

It's just a few simple chords, that's all...

Loci and Constructions

Don't let a silly word like locus put you off — there are easy marks to be had here, but you've got to do everything neatly, using a pencil, ruler and compasses.

Q1 Copy the rectangle on the right and inside it:

a) draw the locus of points 5 cm from D

b) draw the locus of points equidistant from A and D

c) indicate by an X the point inside the rectangle which is 5 cm from D and equidistant from A and D.

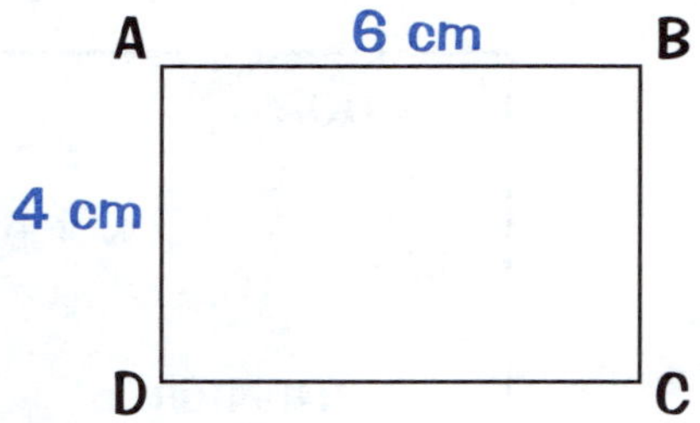

Q2 Construct triangle PQR accurately with length PQ = 10.5 cm, angle PQR = 95° and angle RPG = 32°.

a) Draw in the perpendicular bisector of the line PR. Draw in point A where the bisector crosses the line PQ.

b) Bisect angle PRQ. Draw in point B where the bisector crosses the line PQ. Measure the length BA.

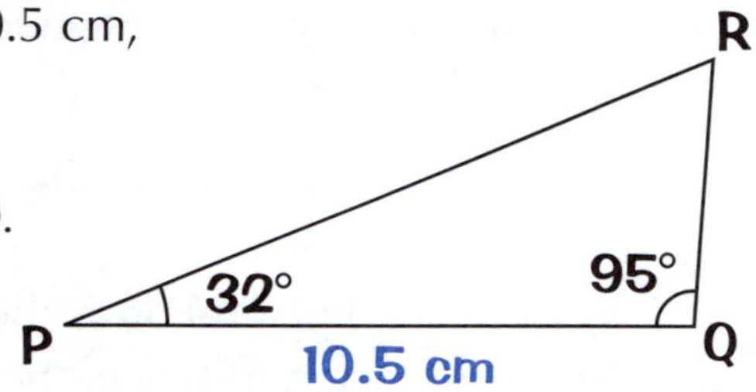

Q3 To win a bet, a man had to walk round his house remaining exactly 3 m from it all the way round.
Using a scale of 1 m to 1 cm draw the locus of the man's movement round the house, marking the walls of the house clearly on your diagram.

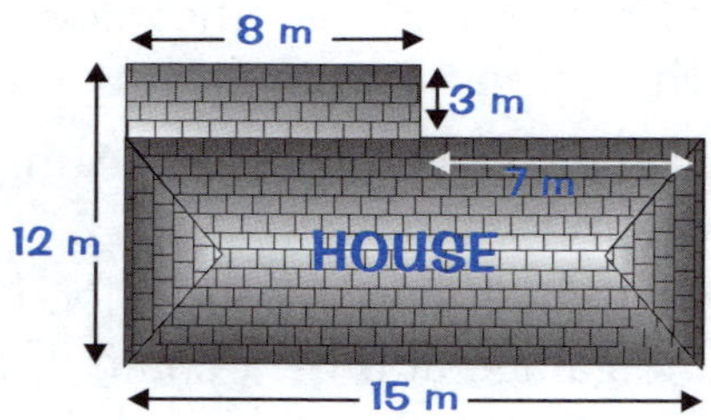

Q4 A and B are 2 points on a straight shore, 4 km apart with A due west of B.

a) Describe the locus of points P such that angle APB equals 90°.

b) Using a scale of 2 cm to 1 km draw an accurate scale diagram showing A, B, the shore line and the locus of P.
An outcrop of rock is located on a bearing of 060° from A and 300° from B.

c) Indicate the rock on your diagram. Mark the spot with an X.

d) A ship steaming due east parallel to the shore avoids the rock by following the locus of P. How near does the ship come to the rock?

Q5 Construct triangle PQR with length PQ = QR = 11.5 cm and angle PQR = 38°.

a) Draw the bisectors of angles QPR and QRP.
Mark the point O where the 2 bisectors cross.

b) With centre O draw the circle which just touches the sides PQ, PR and QR of the triangle.
What is the radius of this circle?

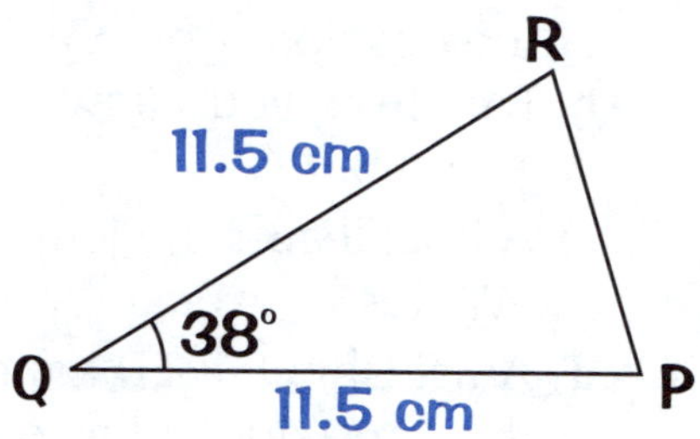

Loci and Constructions

Just to be really awkward, these points don't always make a nice line — they cover a whole area... and you're gonna be asked to shade the area containing all the points.

Q6 This is a plan of Simon's room. To keep warm Simon must be within 2 m of the wall containing the radiator. To see out of the window he must be within 1.5 m of the wall containing the window.

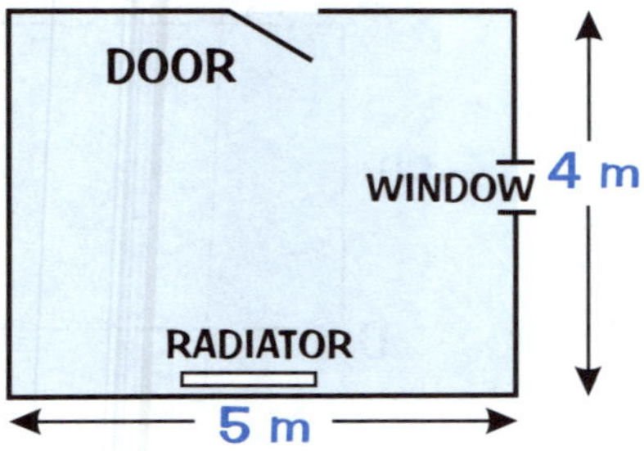

a) Using a scale of 2 cm to 1 m, draw a plan of Simon's room.

b) Shade the region in which Simon must be if he is to be warm and see out of the window.

Q7 A running track is designed so that each point on the track is 32.5 m from a fixed line AB which is 100 m long.

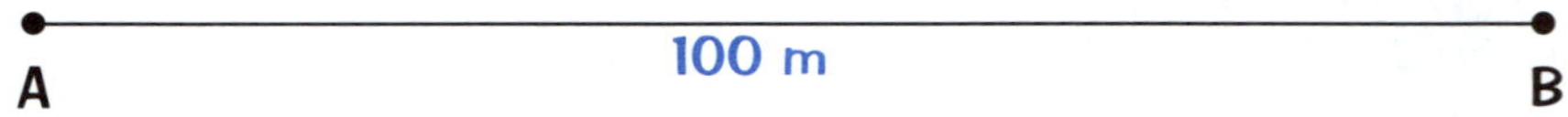

a) Copy the line and draw the locus of the track.

b) Calculate the distance once round the running track.

Q8 The diagram shows a plan of Jim's back garden. Two sides of the garden are bounded by fences and the other sides are bounded by the walls of the house and garage. The garden is in the form of a rectangle.

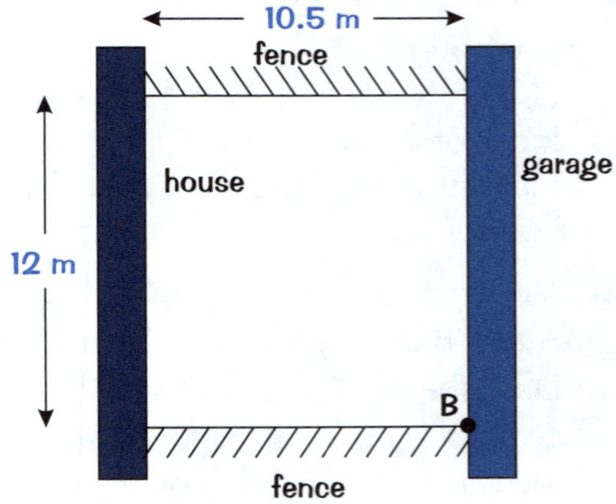

a) Using a scale of 1 cm to 1 m, draw a plan of Jim's garden.

b) Ben, the friendly Rottweiler, is tethered to the garage at B by a chain of length 3 m. Construct accurately and shade the part of the garden where Ben can go.

c) Jim wants to plant a tree in the garden. The tree must be planted more than 5 m away from the walls of the house and more than 4 m away from each fence. On the plan of the garden, construct accurately and shade the region where Jim can plant his tree.

Q9 The positions of two islands A and B are found from the following information: A is 35 km from a jetty J on a bearing 065°, B is due south of A and on a bearing of 132° from J, as shown on the map.

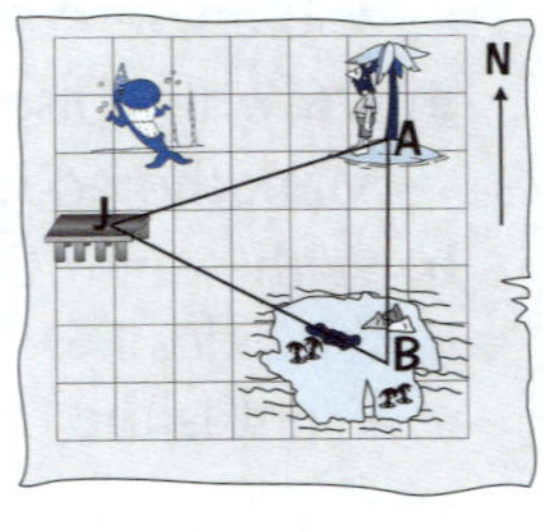

a) Using a scale of 1 cm to 5 km, draw an accurate plan to show the positions of J, A and B.

b) Find from your drawing the distance in km between the islands A and B.

c) A boat leaves the jetty at 0900 and reaches A at 1130. What is its average speed in km/h?

d) A lightship L is 20 km from J, equidistant from A and B and on the same side of J as A and B. Mark L on the drawing.

e) Find the bearing of L from J.

The Four Transformations

Only 4 of these to learn... and good old TERRY's always around to help if you need him.

Q1 Copy the axes and mark on triangle A with corners (–1, 2), (0, 4) and (–2, 4).

Use a scale of 1 cm to 1 unit.

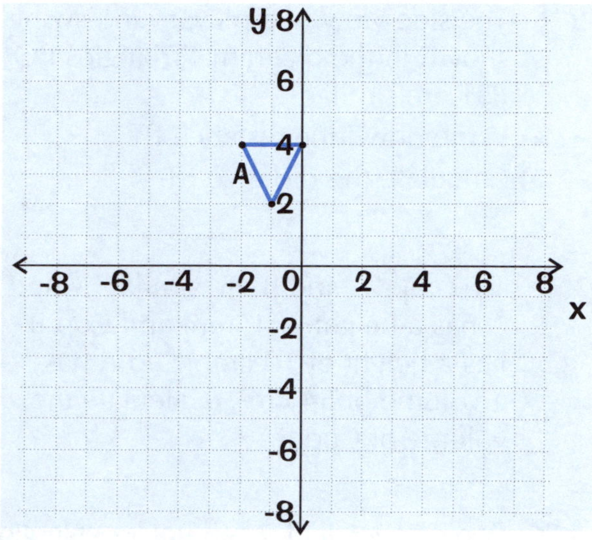

a) Reflect A in the line $y = -x$.
Label this image B.

b) Reflect A in the line $x = 1$.
Label the image C.

c) Reflect A in the line $y = -1$.
Label the image D.

d) Translate triangle D with the vector $\begin{pmatrix}4\\2\end{pmatrix}$. Label this image E.

e) Translate triangle C with the vector $\begin{pmatrix}3\\-3\end{pmatrix}$.
Label this image F.

f) Describe fully the transformation that sends C to E.

g) Describe fully the transformation that sends F to A.

Transformations... just about the most fun you can have without crying.

Q2 Draw axes with x and y running from 0 to 12 with a scale of 1 cm to 1 unit.

O is the origin. $\overrightarrow{OP} = \begin{pmatrix}4\\2\end{pmatrix}$, $\overrightarrow{PQ} = \begin{pmatrix}-1\\2\end{pmatrix}$, and $\overrightarrow{QR} = 2\,\overrightarrow{OP}$

a) Mark P, Q and R on your axes.

b) Calculate the lengths of the vectors $\overrightarrow{OP}$ and $\overrightarrow{OQ}$.

c) Find the equation of the line joining P and Q.

d) Give R the translation $\overrightarrow{QO}$. Label the image T.

e) Verify that the column vectors $\overrightarrow{PQ} + \overrightarrow{QR} + \overrightarrow{RT} + \overrightarrow{TP} = O$.

Urghh — vectors... Make sure you get the coordinates the right way round — top for x dir^n, bottom for y dir^n.

Q3 In the diagram, A is the point (4, 1) B is (5, 1) and C is (4, 3).

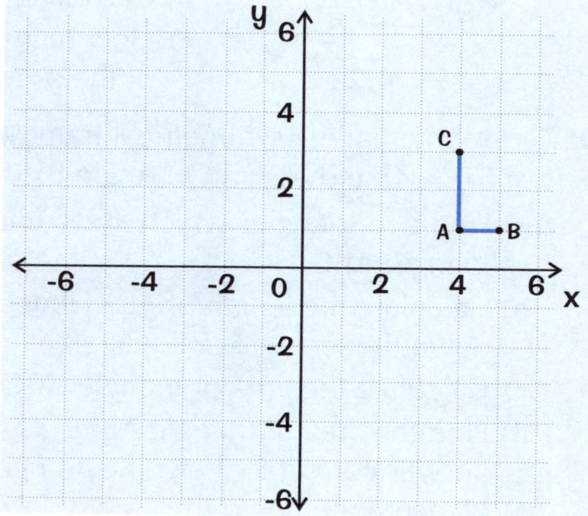

a) Using a scale of 1 cm to 1 unit, draw the diagram and mark on it the figure given by ABC.

b) Reflect ABC in the x-axis and label the image $A_1B_1C_1$.

c) Reflect ABC in the y-axis and label the image $A_2B_2C_2$.

d) Describe fully the single transformation which would map $A_1B_1C_1$ onto $A_2B_2C_2$.

Similarity and Enlargement

There's an important difference between similarity and congruence — make sure you know what it is.

Q1 The side view of a playground swing is shown in the diagram. Triangles PQR and PST are similar.

a) Write down the distance PT.

b) Calculate the distance ST.

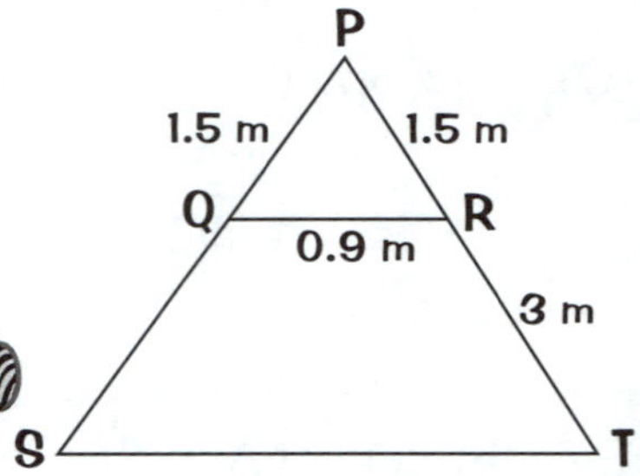

Q2 Two cups A and B are similar. Cup A has a height of 15 cm and Cup B has a height of 10 cm. Cup A has a volume of 54 cm³. Calculate the volume of Cup B.

Don't forget that when you're enlarging areas and volumes, there's a bigger scale factor — that one catches everyone out, believe me...

Q3 A box of chocolates is to have the shape of a cuboid 15 cm long, 8 cm wide and 10 cm high.

a) Calculate the area of material needed to make the box (assuming no flaps are required for gluing).

b) In advertising the chocolates, the manufacturer decides he will have a box made in a similar shape. The enlargement is to have a scale factor of 50. Calculate the area of material required to make the box for publicity. Give your answer in square metres.

Q4 A scale model of a proposed water tower is as shown. The model is a cylinder of height 4 m and base radius 0.2 m. The proposed height of the full-sized tower is 100 m.

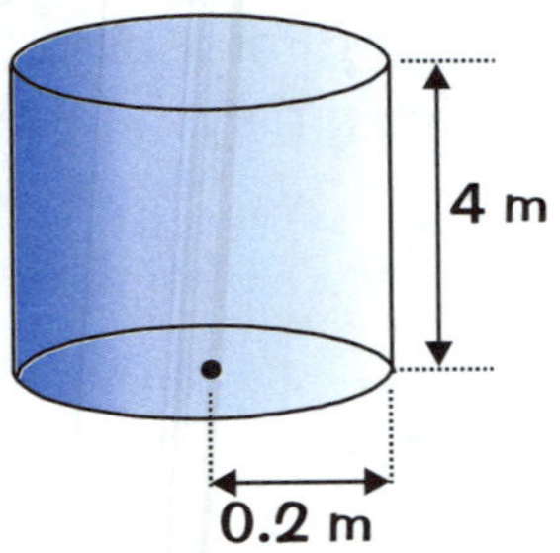

a) What is the base radius of the full-sized tower?

b) Calculate, in cubic metres, the volume of the scale model.

c) How many times larger than the scale model is the volume of the proposed water tower?

Q5 A boy made a symmetrical framework with metal rods as shown. Lengths AB = BC, ST = TC and AP = PQ. Angle BVC = 90° and length BV = 9 cm.

a) Find two triangles which are similar to triangle ABC.

b) Calculate the length of AP. Hence write down the length of PT.

c) Calculate the area of triangle ABC.

d) Find the area of triangle APQ. Give your answer correct to 3 significant figures.

e) Hence write down the area of PQBST correct to 2 significant figures.

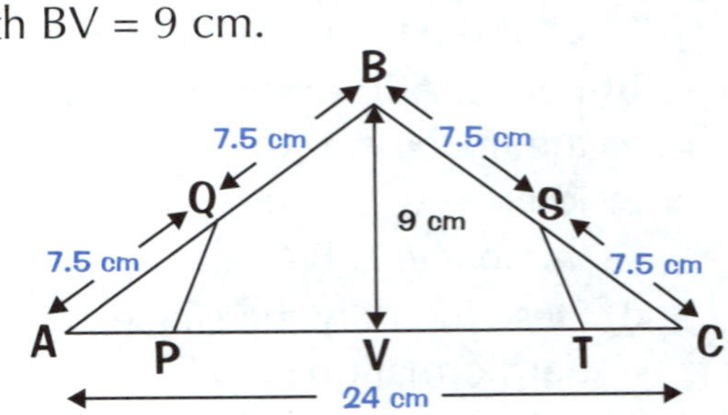

Similarity and Enlargement

Q6 A triangle ABC and a point O are shown on the right. Copy the diagram and, using the point O as centre of enlargement, draw accurately and label:

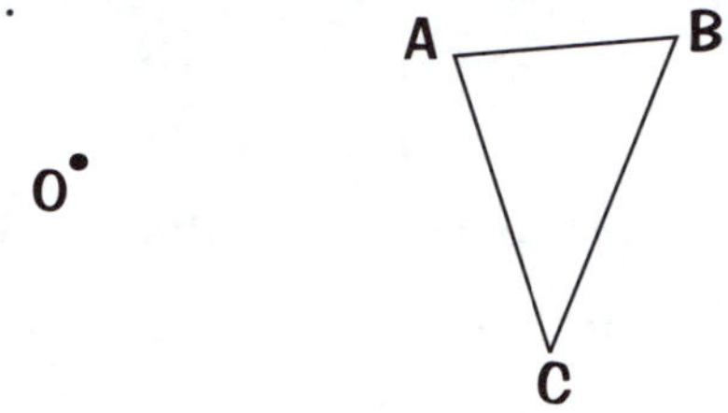

a) the image $A_1B_1C_1$ of the triangle ABC after an enlargement scale factor 2

b) the image $A_2B_2C_2$ of the triangle ABC after an enlargement scale factor –1.

c) Which image is congruent to triangle ABC?

Q7 On a holiday near the sea, children built a sandcastle in the shape of a cone. The radius of the base is 100 cm and the height is 100 cm.

a) What is the volume of the sandcastle in m³ correct to 3 significant figures?

The children now remove the top portion to make a similar cone but only 50 cm in height.

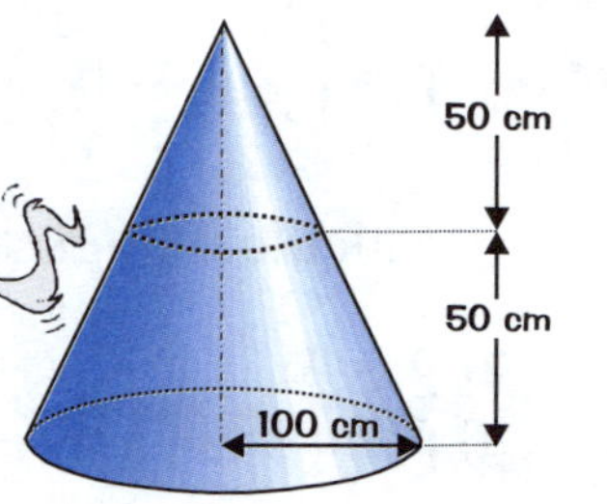

b) State the radius of the base of this smaller cone.

c) State the ratio of the volume of the small cone to the volume of the original cone.

d) Calculate the volume of the small cone in m³ correct to 3 significant figures.

e) Hence write down the ratio of the volume of the portion left of the original cone to the smaller cone in the form n:1.

Q8 A cylindrical bottle contains 1 litre of oil. A second cylindrical bottle has twice the radius but the same height. It also contains oil.

a) Explain why these bottles are not similar.

b) How much oil is in the larger bottle?

Q9 Which pair of triangles below is congruent? Give a reason for your answer.

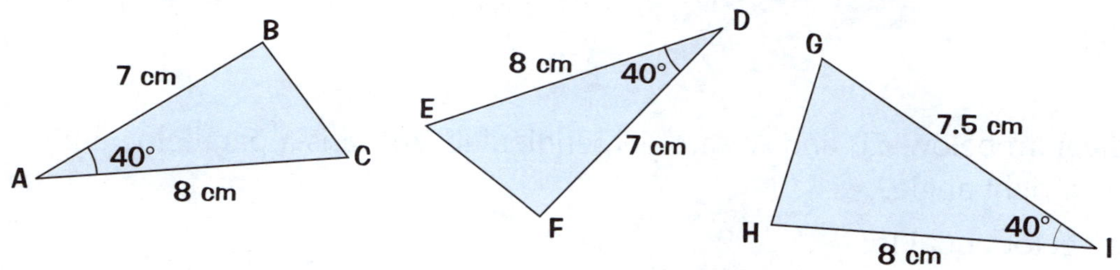

Q10 BC is parallel to DE. AB = 12 cm, BD = 8 cm, DE = 25 cm and CE = 10 cm.

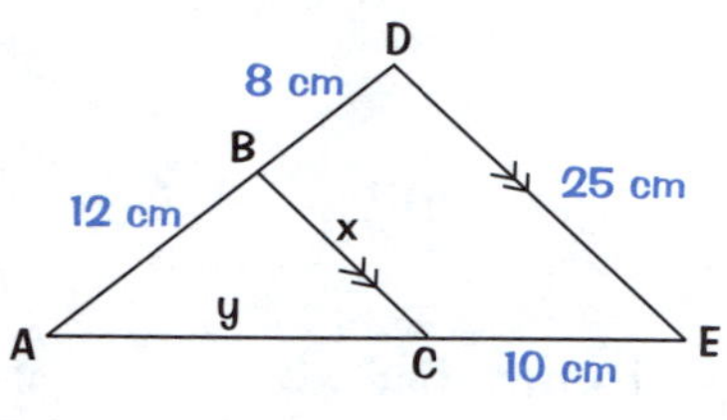

a) Explain why triangles ABC and ADE are similar.

b) Find the lengths of x and y in the diagram.

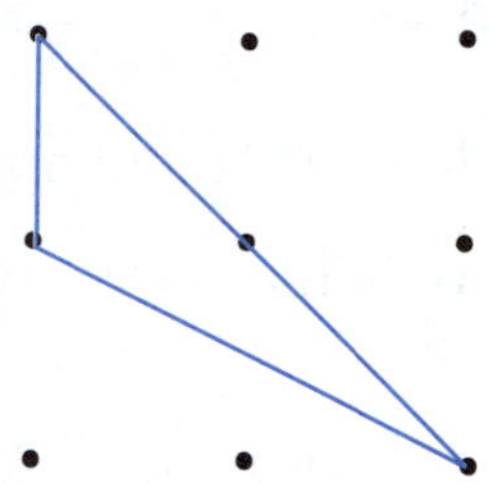

Q11 Another triangle, congruent to the triangle on the right, must be drawn with vertices at three of the dots. Show in how many different ways this can be done.

Vectors

Q1 ABCDE is a pentagon.

$\overrightarrow{AB} = \begin{pmatrix}3\\3\end{pmatrix}$ $\overrightarrow{AC} = \begin{pmatrix}2\\6\end{pmatrix}$ $\overrightarrow{AD} = \begin{pmatrix}-2\\6\end{pmatrix}$ $\overrightarrow{AE} = \begin{pmatrix}-3\\2\end{pmatrix}$

a) Draw this pentagon accurately.

b) Write down the vectors:

i) $\overrightarrow{DE}$ **ii)** $\overrightarrow{DC}$ **iii)** $\overrightarrow{EC}$

c) What sort of triangle is ΔACD?

Q2 $\underset{\sim}{p} = \begin{pmatrix}2\\3\end{pmatrix}$, $\underset{\sim}{q} = \begin{pmatrix}0\\-2\end{pmatrix}$, $\underset{\sim}{r} = \begin{pmatrix}3\\-1\end{pmatrix}$, $\underset{\sim}{s} = \begin{pmatrix}-1\\-2\end{pmatrix}$

Calculate then draw:

a) $\underset{\sim}{p} + \underset{\sim}{q}$
b) $\underset{\sim}{p} - \underset{\sim}{q}$
c) $2\underset{\sim}{r}$
d) $\underset{\sim}{s} + \underset{\sim}{p}$
e) $2\underset{\sim}{p} - 2\underset{\sim}{s}$
f) $3\underset{\sim}{q} + \underset{\sim}{s}$
g) $2\underset{\sim}{r} - \underset{\sim}{q}$
h) $\frac{1}{2}\underset{\sim}{q} + 2\underset{\sim}{r}$
i) $\underset{\sim}{p} + 2\underset{\sim}{s}$
j) $\underset{\sim}{q} - 2\underset{\sim}{r}$

Q3

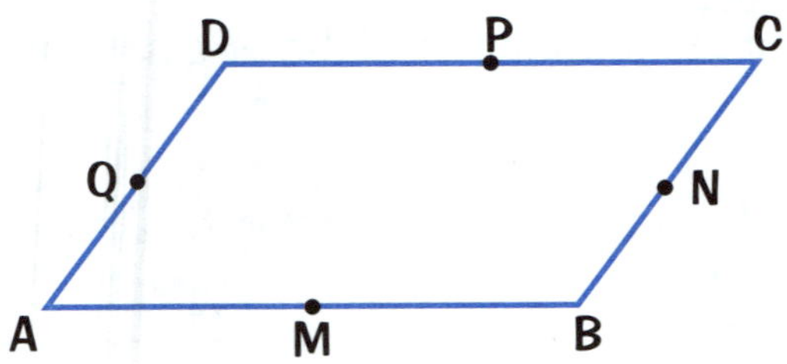

ABCD is a parallelogram.
MNPQ are midpoints of the sides, as shown.
If $\overrightarrow{MQ} = \underset{\sim}{x}$ and $\overrightarrow{AM} = \underset{\sim}{y}$

Express in terms of $\underset{\sim}{x}$ and $\underset{\sim}{y}$:

a) $\overrightarrow{AB}$
b) $\overrightarrow{AQ}$
c) $\overrightarrow{NB}$
d) $\overrightarrow{BC}$
e) $\overrightarrow{AC}$
f) $\overrightarrow{BD}$

Q4 In the diagram below, EB and AC are perpendicular. ABCE is a parallelogram. $\angle$EDC is a right angle.

Name a vector equal to:

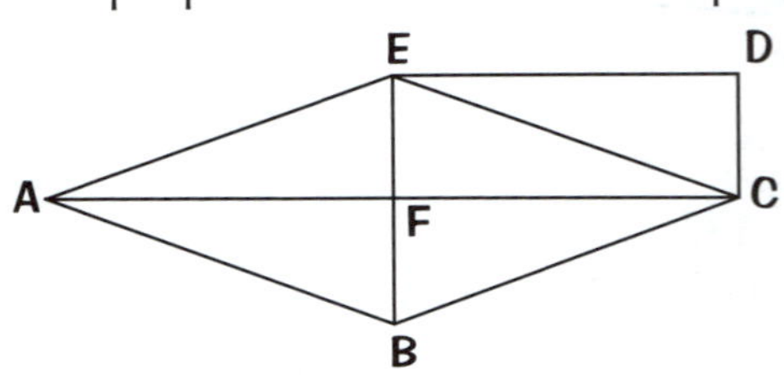

a) $\overrightarrow{FC}$
b) $\overrightarrow{FB}$
c) $\overrightarrow{BC}$
d) $\overrightarrow{CE}$
e) $2\overrightarrow{CD}$
f) $\overrightarrow{AE} + \overrightarrow{EC}$
g) $\overrightarrow{EF} - \overrightarrow{CF}$
h) $\overrightarrow{ED} + \overrightarrow{DC} + \overrightarrow{CB}$

If AC = 16 cm and EB = 6 cm:

i) What is the area of ABCE?
ii) What is the area of ABCDE?

Yep, you're gonna get to practise all that right-angled triangle stuff — Pythagoras, Trig, that sort of thing.

Oh, how the winter evenings will just fly by.

Real-Life Vectors

Look at the pretty pictures... make sure you can see how this little lot fit with the questions, because you'll have to draw your own on the next page.

Q1 In still water my motor boat can achieve 9 km/h. I aim the boat directly across the river which is running at 3 km/h. What is my resultant speed?

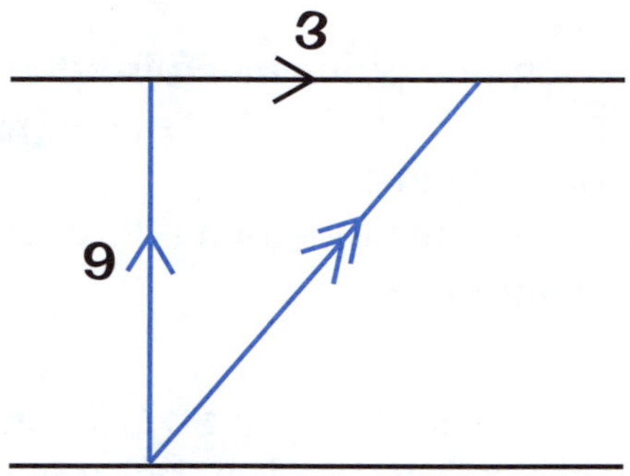

Q2 A girl wants to swim across a river running at 2 km/h. If she can swim at 3.5 km/h, calculate:

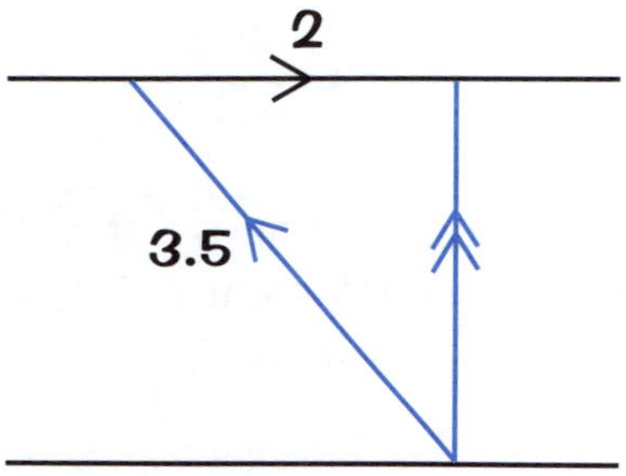

a) at what angle to the bank she should swim to go directly across.

b) her resultant speed.

Q3 An aircraft is attempting to fly due north. It can achieve 600 km/h, but there is a wind from the west at 75 km/h. Calculate:

a) the actual bearing the aircraft is flying on

b) its resultant speed.

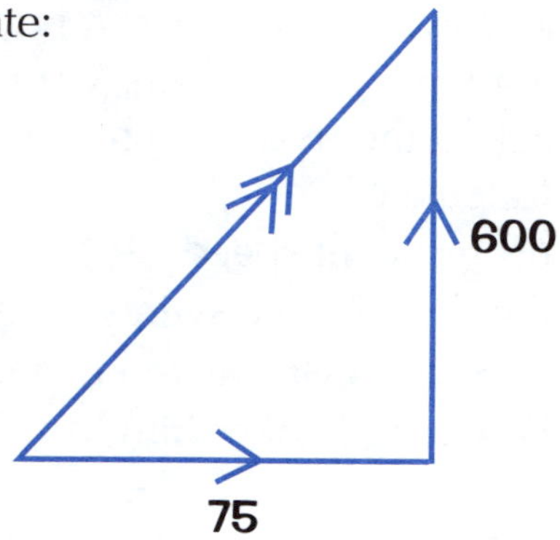

Q4 In the following diagrams the forces are acting on an object as shown.

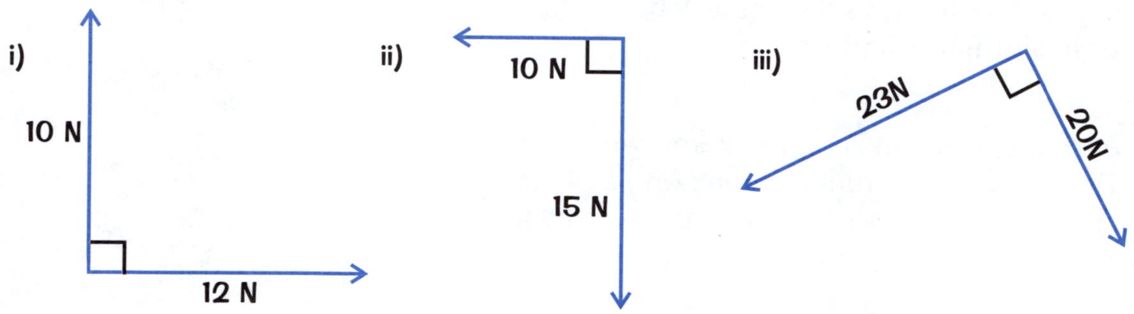

For each find:

a) the resultant force

b) its direction in relation to the larger force.

Real-Life Vectors

For this next one, you've either got to split the vectors into components — F COS θ and F SIN θ, or just add the vectors together end to end and use the Sine and Cosine rules.

It's your call.

Q5 Two tugs are pulling a cruise ship with forces and directions as shown in the diagram.
Find the magnitude of the forward resultant force.

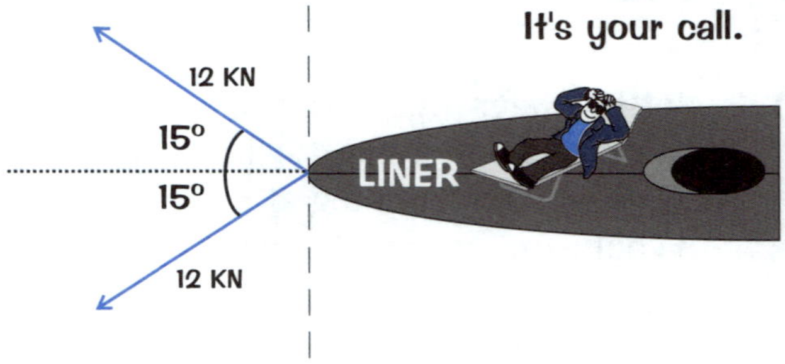

Q6 A helicopter can fly at 80 km/h in still air.
It takes off and heads north-west but is blown off course by a north-easterly wind of 30 km/h.

a) What is its resultant speed?

b) If this helicopter wants to fly north-west, on what bearing should it head?

Q7 A rowing boat needs to reach a point on the opposite bank directly across from its starting point. It can achieve a speed of 5 m/s in still water, but the river runs at 2.5 m/s.
Find the angle with the bank it must make if it is to achieve its objective.

Q8 Two cranes are lifting a bridge girder into place. They exert forces of 65 kN and 75 kN at 24° and 21° to the vertical, respectively.
What is the resultant upward force?

Q9 A river is 16 m wide. A boy who can swim at 2.4 km/h in still water starts to swim from A across the river, which is running at 1.8 km/h.
Calculate:

a) his resultant speed

b) the direction he swims in relation to the bank

c) how far downstream he lands

d) how long it takes him.

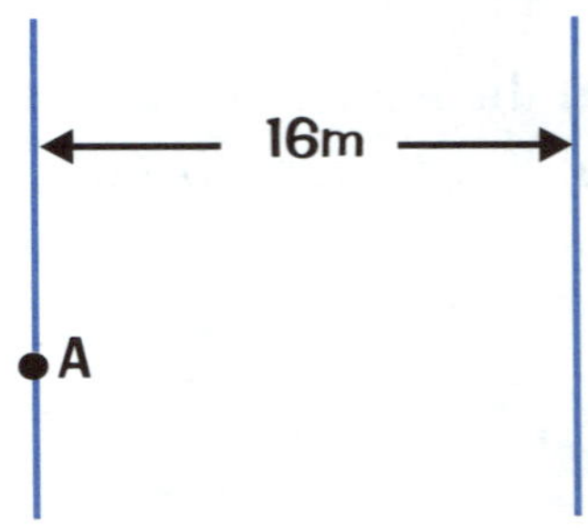

Q10 A Christmas tree is suspended in front of a building by two wires at 45° and 35° to the horizontal. If the tensions in the wires are equivalent to a force of 50 N vertically, find S and T.

Q11 A sailing boat can achieve 12 km/h in still water.
There is a current running due north at 4 km/h.
The boat wishes to sail north-east. Calculate:

a) the bearing it should set to achieve this

b) the resultant speed obtained.

Q12 An aircraft is flying on a course of 290° at 350 km/h. The wind is blowing and the aircraft actually flies on a bearing of 305° at 400 km/h.
Calculate the speed and direction of the wind.

Pythagoras' Theorem and Bearings

Don't try and do it all in your head — you've got to label the sides or you're bound to mess it up. Go on, get your pen out...

Q1 Find the length of the hypotenuse in each of the following triangles:

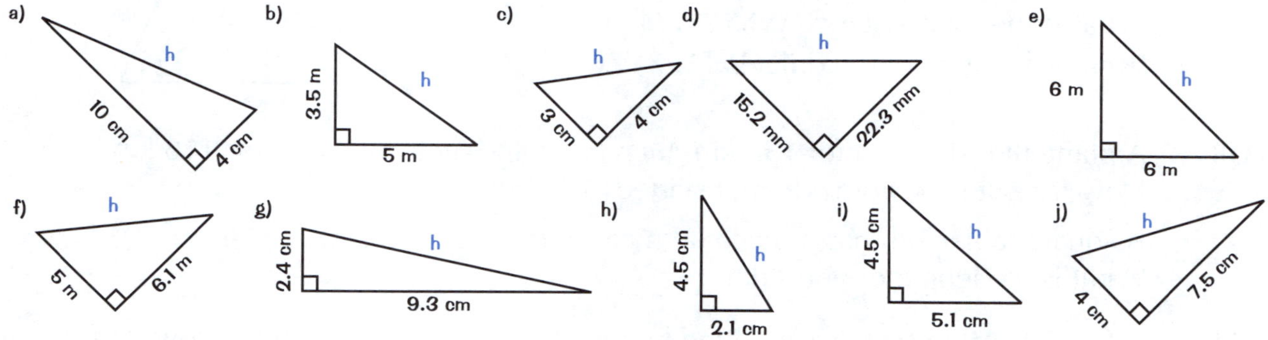

Q2 Find the length of the shorter side in each of the following triangles:

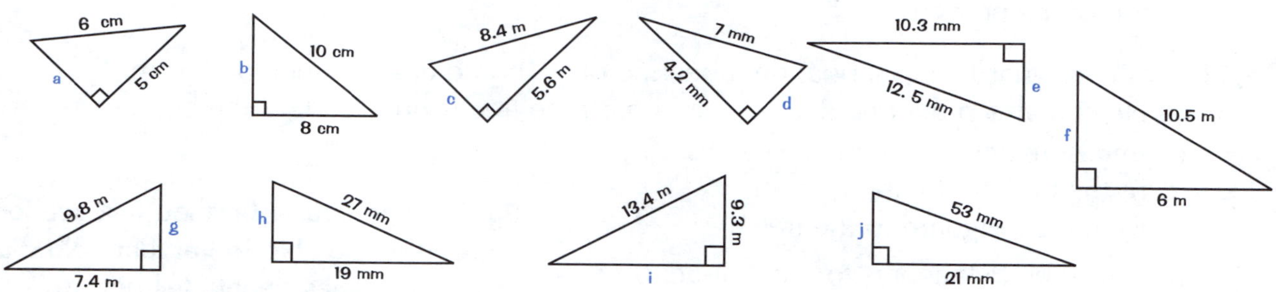

Q3 Find the unknown length in each of the following triangles:

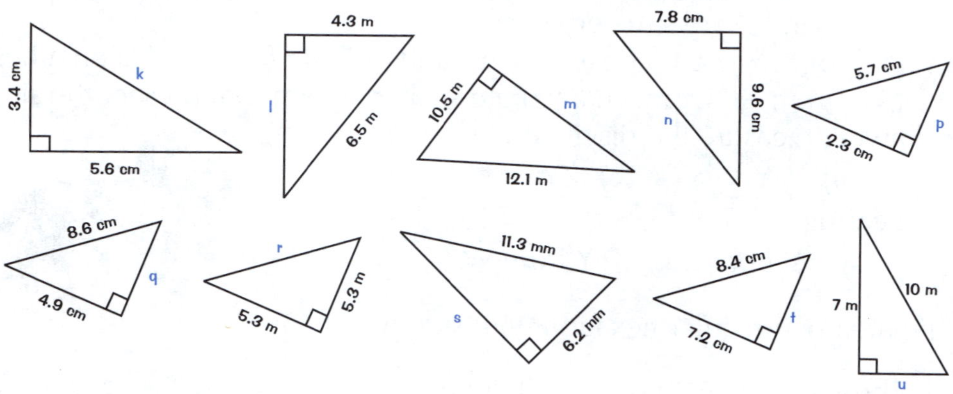

Q4 Find the bearings required in these diagrams:

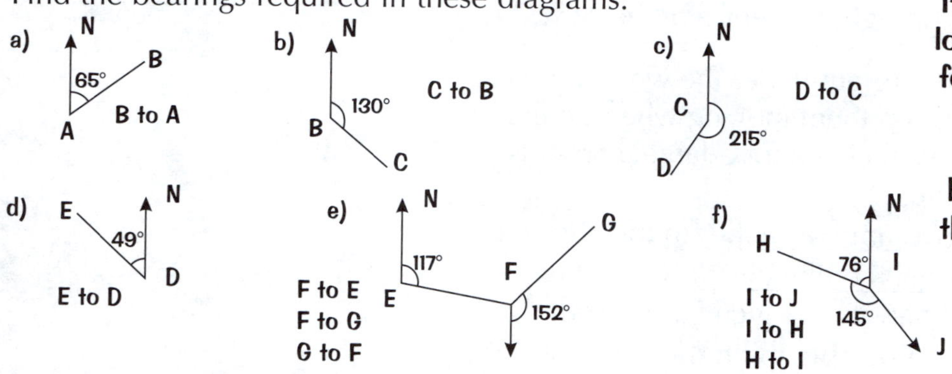

It's easy to get lost if you don't follow the easy rule: always measure bearings from the <u>North Line</u>.

Pythagoras' Theorem and Bearings

Q5 A ladder 11 m long leans against a wall. If the foot of the ladder is 6.5 m from the wall, how far up the wall will it reach?

Q6 A rectangular field is 250 m by 190 m. How far is it across diagonally?

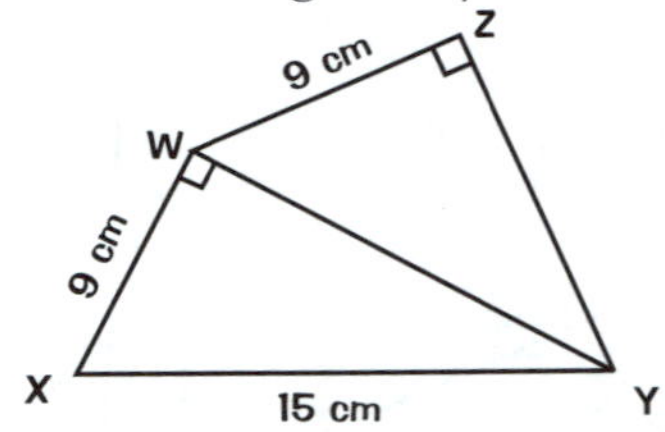

Q7 **a)** Calculate the lengths WY and ZY in the diagram.
b) What is the total distance WXYZW?
c) What is the area of quadrilateral WXYZ?

Q8 A plane flies due east for 153 km, then turns and flies due north for 116 km. How far is it now from where it started?

Q9 A square tablecloth has a diagonal measurement of 130 cm. What is the length of one side?

Q10 A flagpole 10 m high is supported by metal wires each 11 m long. How far from the foot of the pole must the wires be fastened to the ground if the other end is attached to the top of the pole?

Q11 A coastguard spots a boat on a bearing of 040° and at a distance of 350 m. He can also see a tree due east of him. If the tree is due south of the boat:
a) measure accurately the distances of:
i) the boat to the tree.
ii) the coastguard to the tree.
b) Check by Pythagoras to see if your answers are reasonable.

By the time you've finished this section, you'll never be able to get lost. No matter how many times people tell you to.

Q12 Four towns W, X, Y and Z are situated thus:
W is 90 km north of X, Y is on a bearing 175° and 165 km from X, X is on a bearing 129° and 123 km from Z. Draw an accurate scale diagram to represent the situation.
From your drawing measure the distances:
a) WZ **b)** WY **c)** ZY.
Measure the bearings of:
d) Y from Z **e)** W from Z **f)** Y from W.

Q13 Calculate the area of a regular hexagon with side 6 cm.

Q14 A rectangular box measures 20 cm by 30 cm by 8 cm. Calculate the lengths of:
a) the diagonal of each rectangular face
b) the diagonal through the centre of the box.

Q15 Rubber chocks are put under the wheels of aeroplanes to stop them moving when on the ground. A typical chock for a large aircraft is shown opposite.
a) Calculate the volume of rubber in the chock.
b) Calculate the mass of the chock if a rubber compound of density 1.7 g/cm^3 was used.
c) Would a person be able to lift this into position?

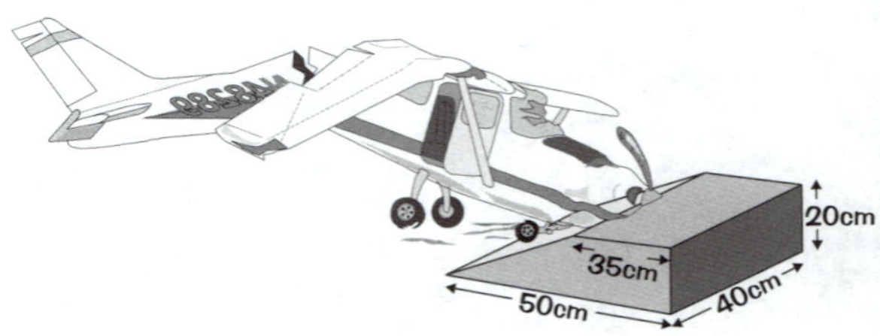

Pythagoras' Theorem and Bearings

Q16 The coordinates of four points are A(2,1), B(6,4), C(7,0) and D(3,–3). Calculate the distances:

a) AB **b)** BC **c)** CD **d)** BD **e)** AC

f) What shape is ABCD?

ahh... nice 'n' easy...

Q17 A plane flies 240 km from A to B on a bearing of 155°.
C is due south of A and 315 km from A.

a) From a scale drawing measure:

i) the bearing of C from B

ii) the bearing of B from C

iii) distance BC.

b) If the plane flies from A to B to C and back to A, calculate the total distance flown.

Make sure you only use Pythagoras on right-angled triangles — it doesn't work too well on anything else. In fact it doesn't work at all.

Q18 A $4\frac{1}{2}$ m ladder is put up against a wall to just reach a window 2.5 m from the ground. How far away from the base of the wall must the bottom of the ladder be?

Q19 A ship sails on a bearing of 300° for 185 km. It is now 110 km due west of a lighthouse. By measuring from a scale drawing, find its distance and bearing from the lighthouse when it started its journey.

Q20 Find the area of an isosceles triangle with these side measurements:

a) 4 cm, 4 cm, 4 cm

b) 9.5 cm, 9.5 cm, 10 cm

c) 15.3 cm, 15.3 cm, 22.7 cm.

Q21 Find the length of line MN, where M and N have coordinates:

a) M(6,3) N(2,8)

b) M(1,5) N(8,12)

c) M(0,1) N(7,3)

d) M(9,5) N(4,8)

e) M(10,4) N(10,0)

f) M(12,6) N(13,0)

Q22 Find the length of line PQ, where P and Q have coordinates:

a) P(2,–3) Q(3,0)

b) P(1,–8) Q(4,3)

c) P(0,–1) Q(2,–3)

d) P(–6,–1) Q(7,–9)

e) P(12,–3) Q(–5,5)

f) P(–10,–2) Q(–2,–8)

OK, so there's a few negative numbers creeping in here, but they're really no harder.

Trigonometry

Before you start a trigonometry question, write down the ratios, using SOH CAH TOA (Sockatoa!) — it'll help you pick your formula triangle.

Q1 Use the tangent ratio to find the unknowns:

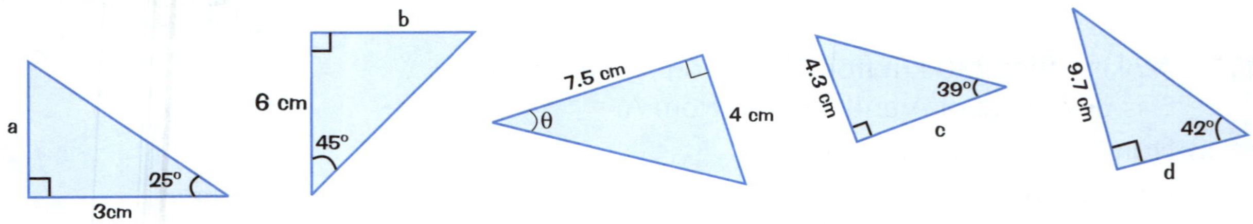

Q2 Use the cosine ratio to find the unknowns:

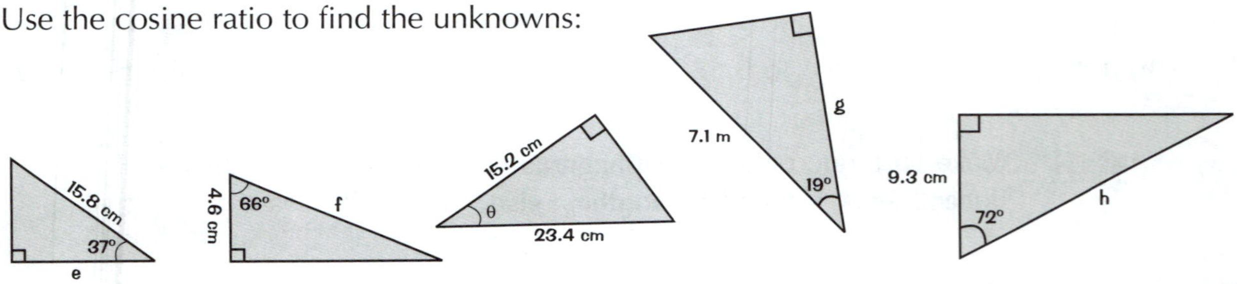

Q3 Use the sine ratio to find the unknowns:

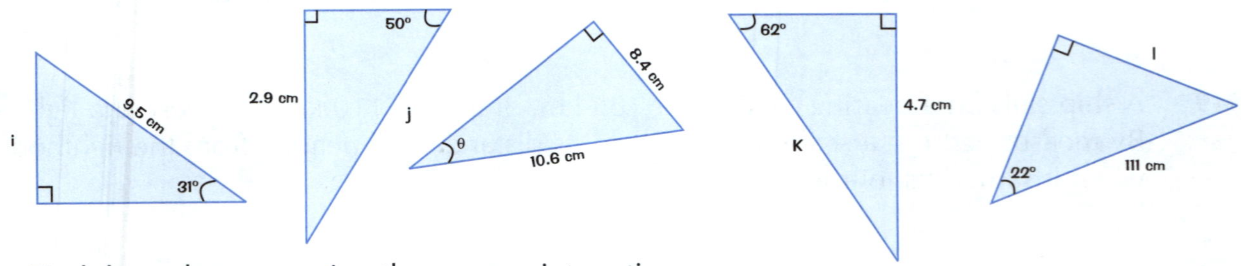

Q4 Find the unknowns using the appropriate ratios:

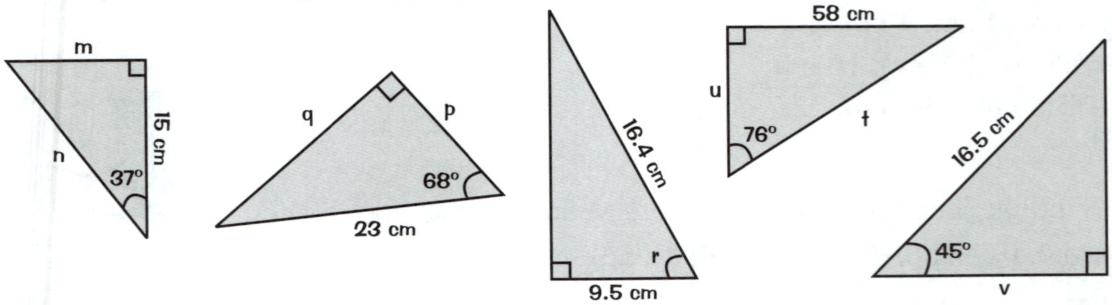

Q5 Calculate the tan, sin and cos of each of these angles:
a) 17° **b)** 83° **c)** 5° **d)** 28° **e)** 45°.

Q6 Calculate the height of the tree using the measurements in the diagram:

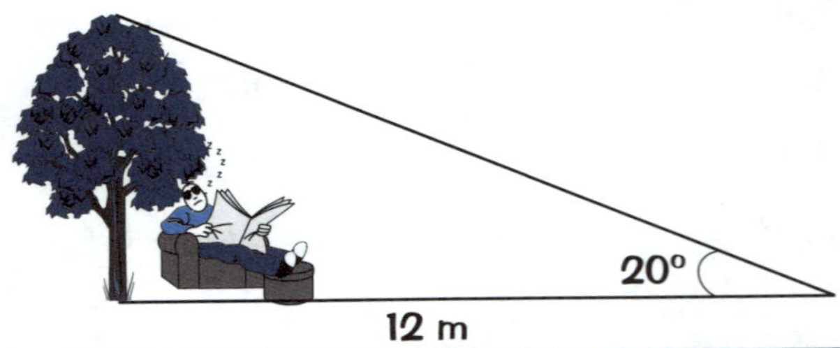

Trigonometry

Q7 A boat travels 9 km due south and then 7 km due east. What bearing must it travel on to return to base?

Make sure you've got the hang of the inverse SIN, COS and TAN functions on your calc... and check it's in DEG mode or you'll get nowhere fast.

Q8 An isosceles triangle has two equal sides of 7 cm and an angle between them of 65°. Calculate the area of the triangle.

Q9 The isosceles triangle opposite has a base of 28 cm and a top angle of 54°. Calculate:

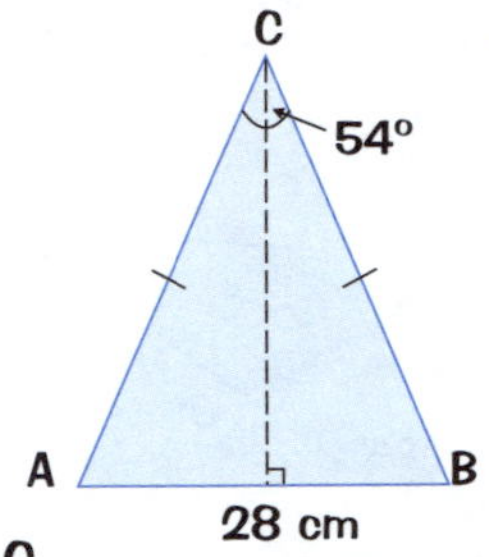

a) the length of sides AC and BC
b) the perpendicular height to C
c) the area of the triangle.

Q10 In this parallelogram the diagonal CB is at right angles to AC. AB is 9.5 cm and ∠CAB is 60°. Calculate:
a) CB **b)** BD **c)** the area of the parallelogram.

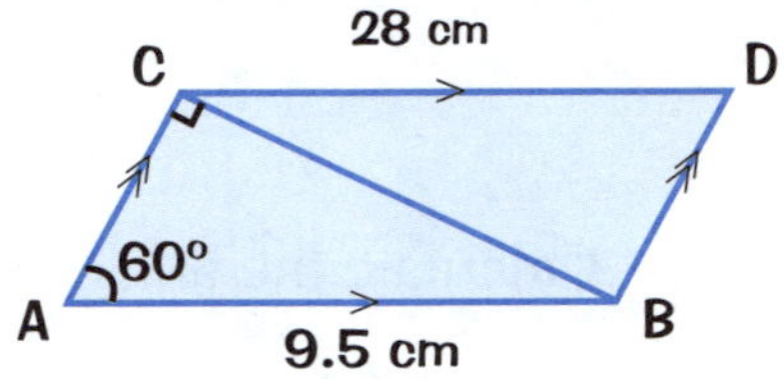

Q11 This rhombus WXYZ has base 15 cm and diagonal WY of 28 cm. Calculate the:
a) length of diagonal XZ
b) area of the rhombus
c) angle WY makes with WX.

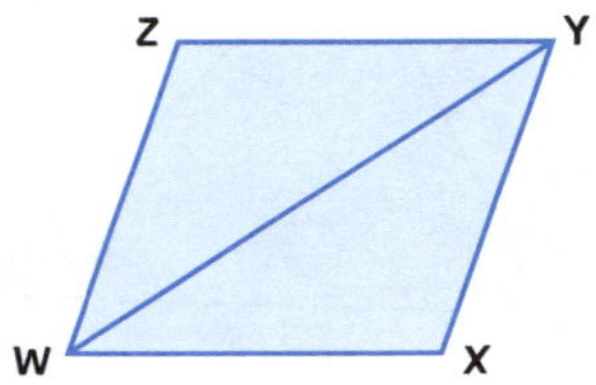

Q12

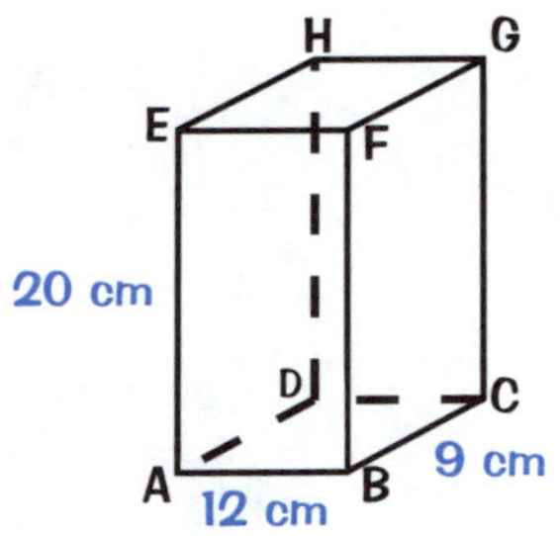

This rectangular box is 20 cm by 12 cm by 9 cm. Calculate:
a) angle ∠FAB
b) length AF
c) length DF
d) angle ∠AFD

Q13 A girl flies a kite on a 45 m long string, which is held 1.3 m above the ground. The string of the kite makes an angle of 33° with the horizontal. What is the vertical height of the kite from the ground?

Q14 I am looking from the top of an 80 m high tower. I look due north and see two cars with angles of depression of 38° and 49°. Calculate:
a) how far each car is from the base of the tower
b) how far apart the cars are.

Q15 This cone has a perpendicular height of 9 cm. The centre of the base is O. The slant line from X makes an angle of 23° with the central axis. Calculate:
a) the radius of the base
b) the area of the base
c) the volume of the cone.

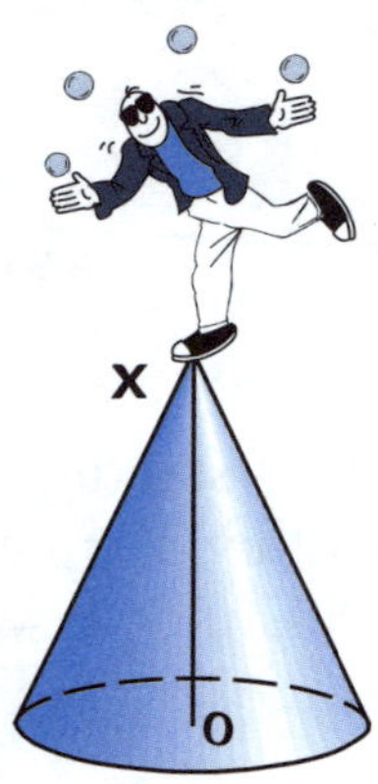

The Sine and Cosine Rules

Make sure you know the Sine Rule and <u>both forms</u> of the Cosine Rule. You won't stand a chance in the exam otherwise.

Q1 Calculate the lengths required to 3 s.f.:

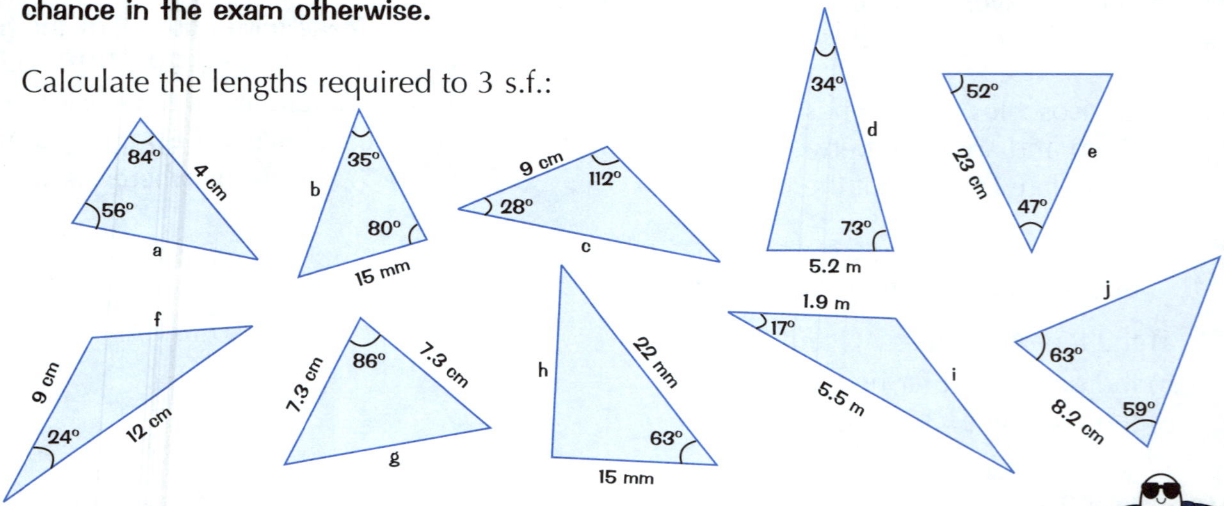

Q2 Calculate the angles required, to the nearest degree:

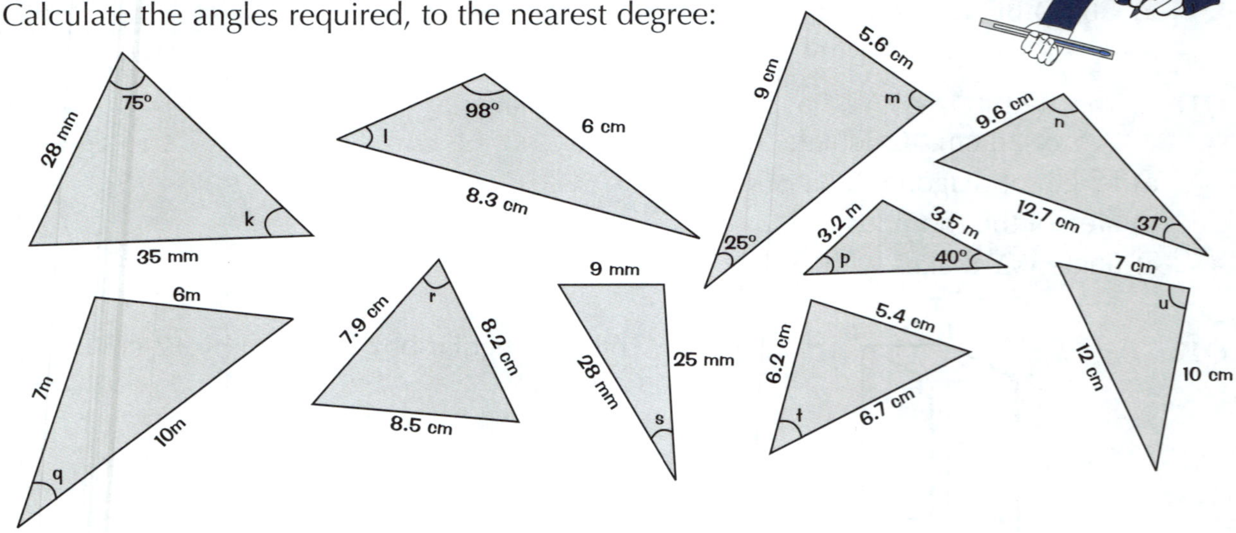

Q3 Calculate the lettered sides and angles:

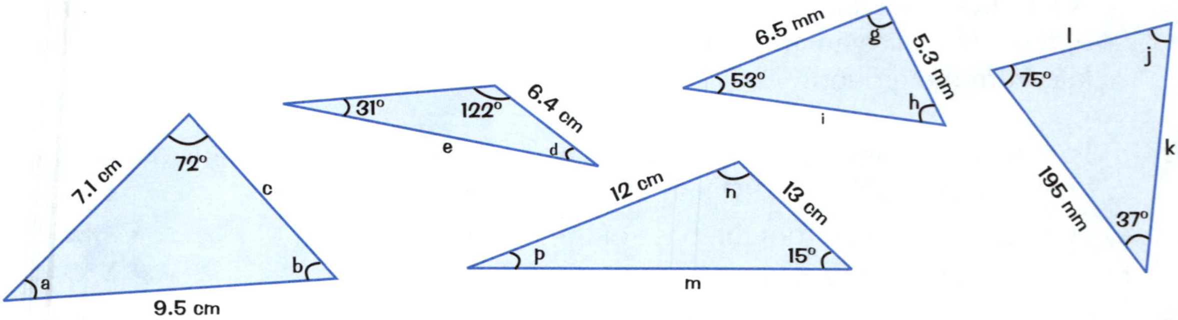

Q4 Peter is standing on a bridge over a river. He can see a tree on each bank, one 33 m and the other 35 m away from him. If he looks through an angle of 20° going from one tree to the other, how far apart are the two trees?

The Sine and Cosine Rules

Q5 A coastguard sees a boat on a bearing of 038° from him and 25 km away. He also sees a ship 42 km away and on a bearing of 080°. Calculate:

a) the distance of the boat from the ship

b) the bearing of the boat from the ship.

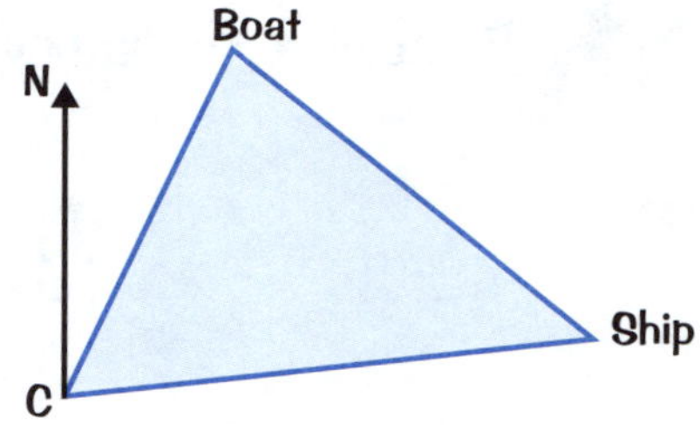

Q6 A triangular field has measurements as shown. Calculate:

a) ∠ZXY

b) ∠XYZ

c) ∠YZX

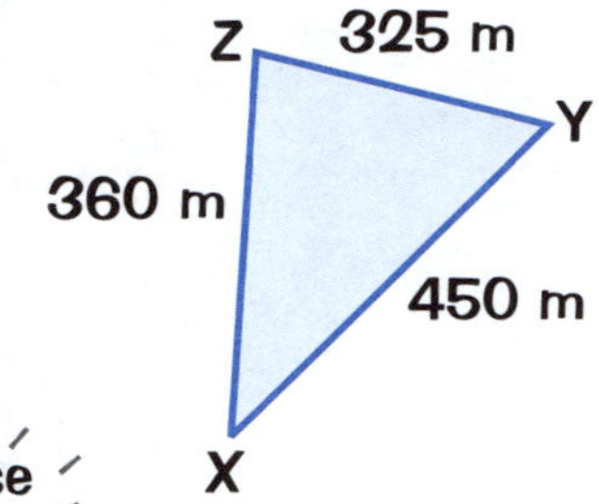

If you don't know which to use, try the Sine Rule first, because it's easier. Normally you won't have much choice, though.

Q7 An isosceles triangle has equal sides of length 7.5 cm and an angle of 56°. Sketch two possible triangles using this information and calculate the two answers for the length of the third side.

Q8 A parallelogram has sides of length 8 cm and 4.5 cm. One angle of the parallelogram is 124°. Calculate the lengths of the two diagonals.

Q9 On my clock the hour hand is 5.5 cm, the minute hand 8 cm and the second hand 7 cm, measured from the centre. Calculate the distance between the tips of the:

a) hour and minute hands at 10 o'clock

b) minute and second hands 15 seconds before 20 past the hour

c) hour and minute hands at 1020.

Q10 A vertical flagpole FP has two stay wires to the ground at A and B. They cannot be equidistant from P, as the ground is uneven. AB is 22m, ∠PAB is 34°, ∠PBA is 50° and A and B are level with P . Calculate the distances:

a) PA

b) PB.

If the angles of elevation of F from A is 49°, calculate:

c) FA

d) PF.

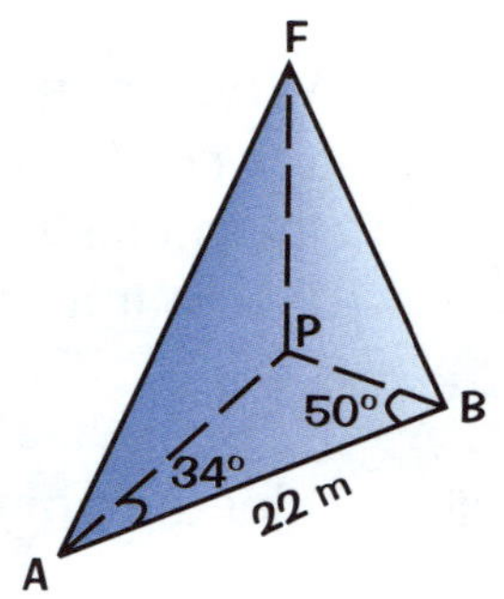

Q11 An aircraft leaves A and flies 257 km to B on a bearing of 257°. It then flies on to C, 215 km away on a bearing of 163° from B. Calculate:

a) ∠ABC

b) distance CA

c) the bearing needed to fly from A direct to C.

Q12 Mary and Jane are standing one behind the other flying a kite with two strings. Each girl has one string. Both strings are held at the same height. The angles of elevation of the kite from the girls are 65° and 48° respectively. If Jane is 2.3 m behind Mary, calculate the length of each string.

The Graphs of Sin, Cos and Tan

Remember — Sin and Cos only have values between –1 and 1.

Q1 This is the graph of $y = \sin(x)$. Write down the coordinates of the points A, B and C.

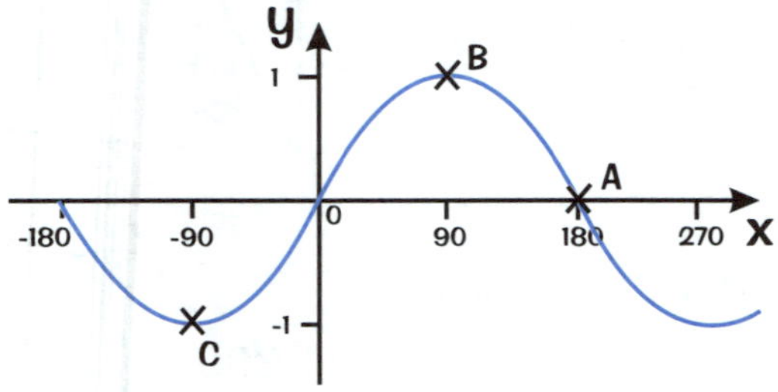

Q2 This is the graph of $y = \cos(x)$. Write down the coordinates of the points D, E, F and G.

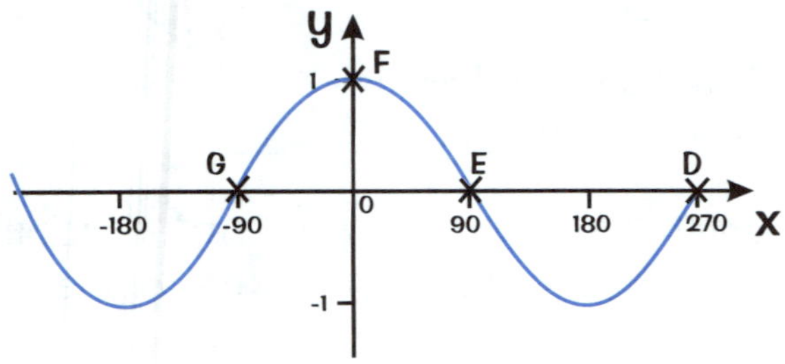

Q3 To the right is the graph of $y = \tan(x)$.
Write down the coordinates of the points H, I, and J.

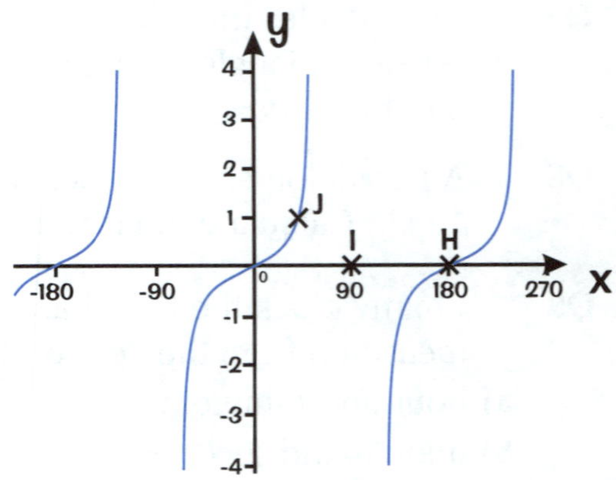

Don't forget — something strange happens with Tan at 90°, 270°, 450° etc. — it shoots off to + infinity... still, at least it comes back again (even if it is from – infinity.)

Q4 Which of the graphs $y = \sin(x)$, $y = \cos(x)$, $y = \tan(x)$ go through the points labelled A, B, C, ...J? (Sometimes it is more than one).

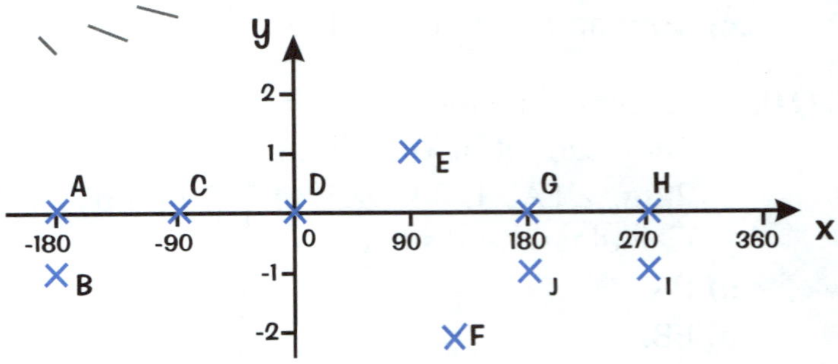

Q5 Plot the points given in this table:

x	0	90	180	270	360
y	2	1	0	1	2

Write down an equation for the curve you have plotted.

Q6 Draw the curve of:

a) $y = \sin(2x)$

b) $y = 2\sin(2x)$ for $0° \leqslant x \leqslant 360°$.

Q7 Draw the curve of $y = 1 + \cos(x)$ for $-180° \leqslant x \leqslant 180°$.

The Graphs of Sin, Cos and Tan

Q8 Draw the curve of $y = -\sin(x)$ for $0° \leqslant x \leqslant 360°$.
What transformation is this of $y = \sin(x)$?

Q9 Draw accurately the graph of $y = 10\cos(x)$ for $-180° \leqslant x \leqslant 180°$.
On the same axes draw the graph of $10y = x + 20$.
Write down the coordinates of the point where the graphs cross. Show that this can be used to find a solution to the equation:

$$20 = 100\cos(x) - x.$$

Q10 Complete this table of values for $\sin(x)$ and $(\sin(x))^2$:

X	0	10	20	30	40	50	60	70	80	90
sin x		0.17		0.5						1
$(\sin x)^2$		0.03		0.25						1

Draw axes for the graph from $-180° \leqslant x \leqslant 180°$.
Plot the points for $(\sin(x))^2$.
From your knowledge of sin graphs, draw the rest of the graph for the limits given.

Q11 Draw accurately the graph of $y = \tan(x)$ for $0° \leqslant x \leqslant 360°$. Let the y-axis have values -10 to $+10$.
On the same axis, draw the graph of $10y - x = 25$.
Use your graphs to find an approximate solution to the equation $x = 10\tan(x) - 25$.

Q12 Draw a table of points to plot $y = \tan(x) + \sin(x)$:

a) for $-90° \leqslant x \leqslant 90°$

x	-90	-70	-50	-30	-10	0	10	30	50	70	90
tan x		-2.75			-0.18			0.58			
sin x		-0.94			-0.17			0.5			
y		-3.69			-0.35			1.08			

b) for $90° \leqslant x \leqslant 270°$.

x	90	110	130	150	180	200	220	240	270
tan x			-1.19						
sin x			0.77						
y			-0.42						

c) Sketch the shape of the graph for $-90° \leqslant x \leqslant 270°$.
Why did you need to plot such a wide range of points?

Angles of Any Size

Q1 The graph of $y = \sin(x)$ is shown below for $-720° \leqslant x \leqslant 720°$.

Graph of y = sin x -720 ≤ x ≤ 720

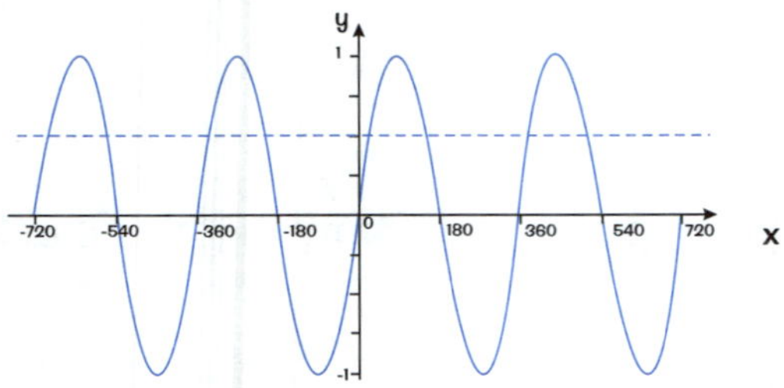

The dotted line drawn at $y = 0.5$ gives values of x as:

$-690°, -570°, -330°, -210°, 30°, 150°, 390°, 510°$.

Write down all the values of x between $-720°$ and $+720°$ when:

a) $\sin(x) = -0.5$ **b)** $\sin(x) = 0.1$ **c)** $\sin(x) = -0.9$.

Remember — the Cos graph is symmetrical about the line $x = 0$, but the Sin graph isn't — it might seem obvious now, but you can guarantee it won't in the Exam.

Q2 The graph of $y = \cos(x)$ is shown below for $-720° \leqslant x \leqslant 720°$. The dotted line drawn at $x = 26°$ shows $\cos(26°) = 0.9$.

Write down all the other angles between $-720°$ and $+720°$ when:

a) $\cos(x) = 0.9$

b) $\cos(x) = 0.5$

c) $\cos(x) = -0.6$.

d) Explain why the positive and negative values are the same for cos, but not for sin.

Graph of y = cos x -720 ≤ x ≤ 720

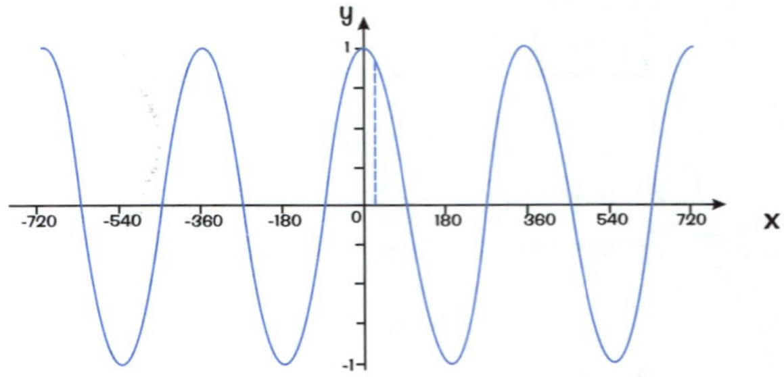

Q3 The graph of $y = \tan(x)$ is shown below for $-450° \leqslant x \leqslant 450°$.

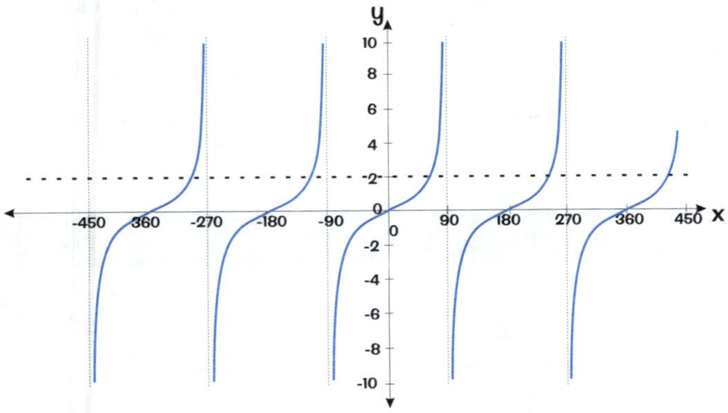

The dotted line drawn where $y = 2$ gives the values of x as: $-297°, -117°, 63°, 243°, 423°$.

Write down all the values of x between $-450°$ and $450°$ to the nearest degree when:

a) $\tan(x) = -1$ **b)** $\tan(x) = 0.5$ **c)** $\tan(x) = 3$.

Q4 Write down the sine, cosine and tangent of each of these angles to 3 s.f.:

a) 175°

b) −175°

c) 405°

d) −735°.

e) What do you notice about the answers to **a)** and **b)**?

f) Can you explain what you notice?

MAHW41